BURGER PARTIES

Featuring Winning Recipes from Sutter Home Winery's
Build a Better Burger® Contest

BURGER PARTIES

James McNair and Jeffrey Starr
Photography by Dan Mills

TEN SPEED PRESS
Berkeley

CONTENTS

PARTY TIME

A great burger is reason enough for a party!
For many of us, life just doesn't get any better than
biting into a big, juicy burger. When all the components are perfect—a patty that's charred on
the outside and moist and tender inside, a high-
quality bun that's toasty warm, spreads that are
packed with flavor, toppings that are crisp and
cool and balance the burger with sweet and
acidic flavors—the combination creates a party
in the mouth. It's no wonder that burgers are
America's favorite food and today are more popular than ever.

The celebrations that we've created for your
pleasure are all centered around some of the
best—and most unique—burgers you'll ever
taste. Each was a prizewinner or an outstanding
finalist in Sutter Home Winery's Build a Better Burger® Recipe Contest and Cook-Off. The
annual search for the best home-cooked burgers in America has been going on since 1990,

and James has been head judge ever since the
contest began. Jeffrey has been the culinary
director and executive chef for Sutter Home
Winery and for the contest since 1999. During
those years, we've encountered an amazing
array of creative burgers from good cooks across
the country and have chosen some of the best to
star in this collection.

We've let the burgers guide us in choosing
party themes and offer ideas for creating a festive atmosphere, with suggestions for decorations, table settings, music, and activities. We
developed side dishes and sweet endings to
complement each burger, along with some spir-
ited wine-based cocktails and wine pairings.

All of us at Sutter Home Winery's Build
a Better Burger hope that this book provides
inspiration for fun celebrations that are perfect
for today's emphasis on relaxed, festive, and
inexpensive entertaining. Let's party!

CREATING FUN PARTIES

Put down that spatula! Before throwing patties on the grill to entertain your friends, you need to do some planning to create a perfect party that is fun for everyone, including yourself.

First, you need to concoct a guest list of compatible people and send out invitations. Draft the guest list to include an interesting mix of friends with shared or dissimilar interests, which can lead to sparkling conversation. Limit the invitees to a number that you can accommodate comfortably. Remember the "old days" of mailing written invitations? Such thoughtfulness still makes a great impression and can go a long way in establishing the party theme. Our fast-paced lives, however, allow for invitations via personal phone calls, e-mails, or online invitation websites. Even text messages may be okay for invitations to very casual, last-minute parties such as Flip 'n' Splash (page 83).

Next, turn your attention to creating the right ambience for the party. "Staging" a party with creative, fun decorations and tableware is important to set the mood and atmosphere; our suggestions go for the optimal experience, but you may choose to elaborate further or simplify.

When planning table settings and linens, keep your parties environmentally friendly by choosing washable real dishes, glasses, flatware, and napkins, or buying disposable products that are eco-friendly and biodegradable. Keep in mind that everything on the table doesn't have to match, but the pieces should be compatible. Dishes in white, beige, or earth tones can mix and match with just about anything and any theme. A collection of California pottery plates in various colors always go together, as do mixtures of black and white patterns or collections of hand-painted designs. If you have plenty of room and few budget restraints, you might have fun building a party pantry with dishes that work for various themes and seasons that you can use year after year.

Nice glasses influence our perception of wine and make the experience of drinking seem more pleasurable. If you have room for only one or two sets, choose an all-purpose wine glass or one with a large bowl for reds and one with a bit smaller bowl for whites. Don't forget the European tradition of bistro glasses for wine as an alternative to stemware for casual burger parties.

Be sure to have lots of napkins on hand—the best burgers can be very messy! Dish towels make great oversized napkins for drippy burgers. White napkins are always acceptable, but colorful solids or prints add a festive note.

While it's impossible to beat fresh flowers on the table, consider other options: seasonal fruits or vegetables, potted herbs or flowering plants, a grouping of candles, a collection of seashells, interesting rocks, or other natural elements that enhance the party theme. The photos in this book will give you lots of good ideas.

Music can play a big role in establishing the mood, and choosing it requires some thought and probably a trip to a music store (check "world music" sections for ethnic music) or ordering from an online seller or downloading. For most of the parties in this book, we suggest theme-enhancing music. It's always special to have live music, so if someone in your group plays guitar or another portable instrument, ask him or her to bring it along. Or tune up and dust off your piano, and plan for live entertainment at some point in your gathering. A sing-along is always a fun party activity.

Evening parties can be greatly enhanced by lighting that creates a mood appropriate to the party theme. Light switch dimmers can quickly create a romantic feeling. For outdoor parties, pull out the strings of tiny white lights from your box of Christmas decorations. They can add a lot of atmosphere to a garden all year round, as can tiki torches, hanging paper lanterns, and strings of overhead bulbs. And indoors or out, nothing beats lots of candles adding their special glow to the night.

Once you've chosen your party theme and made a head count, you need to create a shopping list before you hit the grocery store or farmers' market. Choose a party menu with recipes that use ingredients in season, and, when you shop, always look for the best ingredients you can find. If a burger calls for sliced tomatoes, choose vine-ripened ones from the backyard garden or local farmers' market.

When making your shopping list, take note that all the parties and recipes in this collection have been written to serve six people generously. Just scale recipes up for more guests or folks with big appetites. In addition to the shopping list, jot down a quick list of everything that you need to do before the guests arrive so you're not stressed out when it's time to party.

When you're ready to throw the burgers on the grill, you'll want it to be smokin' hot! Be sure you've got enough charcoal or fuel on hand—nothing spoils a party faster than a raw burger. Our burger recipes are written for cooking all the components on the grill, as required in Sutter Home Winery's Build a Better Burger contest rules, but feel free to use your stovetop when prepping your party burgers.

When shopping for wine, keep in mind that a 750-milliliter bottle contains five 5-ounce servings of wine, and a 1.5-liter bottle has twice as many. Plan accordingly for the number of guests you expect. For casual parties you may wish to stock up on individual 187-milliliter bottles.

Okay, you've got the ingredients, you've stocked up on wine, the party site is decorated, and the table is set. Put on an apron and get chopping! Even though many burgers and accompanying recipes in this book have several steps, none of the individual steps is difficult, and most of the prep work can be done well ahead of time. Many of the starters, side dishes, and sweets can be made the day before, allowing you time to devote to the burgers and last-minute details on party day. An hour or so before guests are due, put together the burger ingredients and refrigerate the patties. Just be sure to take the patties out of the fridge half an hour before cooking—throwing a cold patty on a grill can cause it to stick and cook unevenly. (Fish and poultry patties need to stay chilled until just a few minutes before cooking to prevent spoiling.)

Guests are due to arrive soon, so set out glasses and wine, and be sure you've got a corkscrew handy. If you don't store your wines in a wine refrigerator or cool cellar, we recommend following the simple rule of 20/20: thoroughly chill white wines in the refrigerator and remove about 20 minutes before serving, or refrigerate room-temperature red wines for 20 minutes before pouring. Nonalcoholic beverages—water, juice, lemonade, iced tea, or sodas—should also be available with plenty of ice.

Now slip into your party clothes, fire up the grill, start the music, pour yourself a glass of wine, sit down, and relax until your guests arrive.

One last bit of advice: you've taken the effort to create a fun party, and everyone's having a great time, so don't break the spell. Delay most cleanup tasks until the last guest departs.

MAKING BETTER BURGERS

Whether you're making burgers for one of the parties in this book or creating your own burgers, here are some tips that we've developed while working with Sutter Home Winery's Build a Better Burger competition.

Because any ground meat dries out quickly, buy it freshly ground from a reliable butcher on the day you plan to use it; or purchase boneless meat, and grind or mince it just before cooking.

To grind meat at home, cut the meat and any attached fat into 1-inch chunks and place it in the freezer—along with the grinder or food processor bowl and blade—for about 30 minutes. Partially freezing the meat not only is a safety measure but also firms the meat for easier grinding and makes the lean and fat less homogenous, producing moister, less dense patties. If using a meat grinder, put the chilled meat through the cold grinder fitted with a 1/4-inch blade. If using a food processor, place small batches of chilled meat in the cold processor bowl and pulse just until the meat is minced; avoid overprocessing.

To incorporate flavor into every bite, thoroughly mix seasonings into the ground ingredients. Contrary to popular culinary myth, salting ground meat a few minutes before cooking it will not draw out the moisture and create a dry burger. For our tastes, 1 teaspoon of kosher or coarse sea salt to every pound of meat is a perfect ratio, but if you're adding other salty components, reduce the amount of salt you use.

If making beef burgers, keep in mind that the lower the fat content, the less the flavor and the tougher the cooked patty. Ground chuck, usually around 24 percent fat, and other fatty cuts make the best patties.

When using lean meats, add a little ground fat, a bit of chilled wine or broth, and extra seasonings to keep the patties moist and flavorful.

Throughout the patty-making process, the colder you keep the mixing bowl, meat, wine, broth, and other ingredients, the better.

For a lighter texture and tender patties, handle the mixture as little as possible when mixing in seasonings, and mix with a spoon, because using your hands will warm the fat and lead to a drier, denser burger. Rinse your hands under cold running water to cool them before forming patties, and handle the mixture as little as possible to prevent compacting.

Cook patties shortly before serving, and let them rest under a foil tent for a few minutes for the juices to redistribute.

Brush the hot grill rack with vegetable oil before adding patties, to help keep them from sticking. Alternatively, brush the patties with oil before placing them on a hot grill rack.

Place patties directly over the heat source if you want them well charred on the outside and moist and juicy inside. But when grilling patties with a high fat content or dripping marinades, offset them from the fire to prevent flare-ups.

To keep all the delicious juices inside, avoid pressing down on patties with a spatula during cooking.

When topping with cheese, wait until the patties are almost done. Close the grill lid after adding the cheese, to melt it more quickly.

Burgers taste best when the buns are hot and the cut sides are lightly toasted on the grill during the last few minutes.

Once everything is ready, assemble the burgers quickly and serve immediately.

For easier eating, cut each burger in half before serving. If they are loaded with toppings, you may wish to insert a skewer into each burger half before cutting them, to hold everything in place until your guests are ready to pick them up and chow down.

PAIRING WINE WITH BURGERS

Twenty years ago, most people in the United States viewed wine as serious and intimidating, a beverage reserved for special occasions or for dining out. People were hesitant to buy and serve wine unless they were "experts." When going out to dinner, some were afraid to order wine because they might choose the wrong one. Often, diners set aside the wine list and went straight for a more familiar beverage. Wine as a regular choice at home was almost unheard of here, although it was commonly enjoyed in the wine-growing countries of Europe.

The wine business was partly to blame. A mystique was cultivated around the enjoyment of wine, and experts touted rules to create an image of sophistication and luxury. Most of the time even the experts did not agree, but it gave everybody something to do. In 1990, Sutter Home Winery decided to put an end to this nonsense when we created the Build a Better Burger Recipe Contest and Cook-Off. We set out to take the fear factor out of the enjoyment of food and wine. And what everyday food is more familiar and less intimidating than the good old hamburger? You now see gourmet burgers in top restaurants, on television food shows, and on magazine covers—usually accompanied by a glass of wine.

Because the Sutter Home philosophy is to demystify the food and wine experience, the last thing we want to do is to suggest that with any particular burger there is one certain appropriate wine. We all have different tastes. That is why for every party in the book we have recommended several wines that we think you and your guests will enjoy paired with the starring burger and accompaniments. The bottom line is, if you like a certain food with a certain wine, that is really what it is all about.

That said, when it comes to pairing wine with food there is one key principle to remember: food changes the taste of wine. Have you ever brushed your teeth in the morning and then had a sip of orange juice soon after? The sweet toothpaste changes the taste of the orange juice, making it more sour, even bitter, less sweet, and less fruity. Certain foods can have a similar impact on the taste of wine.

If the change is profound, then the wine will not taste its best. Foods that are sweet, spicy (such as chiles), or high in umami (meaty or savory dishes) can all make the taste of wine *stronger*. On the other hand, salt and acidity in food can be a wine's best friend. These tastes make wine taste *milder*; they are less likely to impair the taste of wine and may, in fact, bring out its best.

> ## WHAT IS UMAMI?
>
> Long known in Asia, umami is Japanese for "savory" or "meaty" and is one of our five basic tastes along with sweet, sour, salty, and bitter. It is found in protein-rich foods in the form of amino acid glutamates. Among foods that are high in umami are red meats, shellfish, mushrooms, tomatoes, potatoes, and cheese. Aging, curing, fermenting, and ripening foods increases the concentration of umami.

At the Sutter Home Culinary Center, when chefs prepare foods that are sweet, spicy, and high in umami, they balance the taste of those foods with a little salt or acidity, such as a squeeze of lemon juice, to bring the recipe into taste balance with the wines.

Because burgers dominant in sweet, spicy, or umami tastes, often found in Asian or Latin recipes, can make wines taste stronger, avoid pairing them with the stronger wines. Milder wines, such as Sauvignon Blanc or Pinot Grigio, are good choices. If the food is extremely sweet or spicy, mild wines with a touch of sweetness, such as Riesling, Gewürztraminer, or White Zinfandel, are better yet.

Burgers with classic European tastes, such as those with roots in French, Italian, Spanish, or Mediterranean cuisine, are not typically high in sweet, spicy, or umami tastes and thus will not adversely affect the bigger, stronger wines, such as Cabernet Sauvignon or Merlot.

Use our chart of wine and burger pairings as a general guide. We also list specific wines for appetizers, the main course (burgers and sides), and desserts in each party menu.

WINES	BURGERS
MILD Chenin Blanc, Gewürztraminer, Moscato, Pinot Grigio, Riesling, Sauvignon Blanc, White Zinfandel	Burgers that are sweet, spicy, or high in umami. Especially good with burgers with Asian or Latin flavors, like the **Albuquerque Chicken Burgers** (page 146), **Hawaii Da Kine Burgers** (page 45), and **Sweet-Hot Thai Burgers** (page 84).
MEDIUM Chardonnay, Sutter Home Red, White Merlot, Zinfandel	Burgers that are slightly sweet or spicy. Medium wines pair beautifully with burgers that have a sweet-and-sour relish, condiment, or spread, like the **Fruit of the Vine Burgers** (page 15), **Pineapple Upside-Down Jerk Burgers** (page 107), and **Sweet and Spicy Red Fez Burgers** (page 115).
STRONG Cabernet Sauvignon, Merlot	Burgers that are only very slightly sweet and spicy and are balanced with nice acidity. Reserve these wines for big, robust burgers with bold additions, like bacon, blue cheese, mushrooms, and grilled onions. The **Home on the Range Buffalo Burgers** (page 100), **Opa! Burgers** (page 26), and **Smoky-Sweet Bacon Burgers** (page 63) are good choices with strong wines.

A Place in the Sun
Wine Country–Style Outdoor Lunch

A vineyard . . . a meadow . . . a field . . . a lawn . . . a deck . . . a balcony . . . Pick your own favorite sunny spot, and invite some sun-loving friends for a salute to wine country. All that sunshine may become too much of a good thing after a while, so be sure there's a shade tree, an arbor, or an umbrella close at hand.

Set the table with sunny, colorful dishes and linens. Hand-painted dishes from the wine regions of France, Italy, and Spain are popular in Napa Valley, as is more casual and richly hued pottery from Mexico and California. A simple country-style bouquet of sunflowers or other cheerful summer blooms adds to the sun-drenched theme. And warm, relaxing Spanish or Latin guitar music will complete the wine-country ambience.

Wine, naturally, is the star at any wine-country gathering. Serve those suggested in our menu, or ask guests to bring along a favorite bottle. Then pair the dishes with various wines, and share what works and doesn't work to everyone's taste. Even though you're feasting in the sun, try to serve wine at a proper temperature (page 4) to show it off best.

MENU

Spicy Gazpacho Shooters
with Quick-Pickled Cucumbers

Fruit of the Vine Burgers
with California Relish

Bibb Lettuce and Endive Salad
with Crisp Prosciutto, Pear, Goat Cheese, and Verjus

Summer Pearl Couscous Salad

Sutter Home Sauvignon Blanc
Sutter Home White Zinfandel
Sutter Home Zinfandel

Almond–Olive Oil Cake
with Strawberries

Sutter Home Moscato

Spicy Gazpacho Shooters *with Quick-Pickled Cucumbers*

Enjoy shots of this zesty soup while the burgers are on the grill. Instead of the usual chopped vegetables added to gazpacho, we've topped the shooters with a bit of freshly pickled cucumbers.
Serves 6

Pickled Cucumbers

1/2 cup peeled, seeded, and diced (1/8 inch) cucumbers

1/4 cup unseasoned rice vinegar

1 tablespoon sugar

1 tablespoon minced fresh basil

Gazpacho

2 pounds vine-ripened tomatoes, cored and coarsely chopped

6 tablespoons coarsely chopped green onions, including green tops

1 red bell pepper, seeded and coarsely chopped

1 jalapeño chile, seeded and coarsely chopped

2 teaspoons coarsely chopped garlic

2 tablespoons balsamic vinegar

2 tablespoons freshly squeezed lemon juice

1 teaspoon Louisiana hot sauce

1 1/2 teaspoons kosher or coarse sea salt

1/2 cup mild extra-virgin olive oil

To make the pickles, combine all the ingredients in a small stainless-steel or other nonreactive bowl, cover, and refrigerate for 1 hour.

To make the gazpacho, combine the tomatoes, green onions, bell pepper, chile, garlic, vinegar, lemon juice, hot sauce, and salt in a food processor or blender and puree until very smooth. With the motor running, drizzle in the oil. Pour the mixture through a fine-mesh strainer into a pitcher; extract all the liquid by pressing the mixture with the back of a spoon until it is dry. Discard the solids. Taste and add more lemon juice, hot sauce, and salt, if desired. Cover and chill the gazpacho thoroughly.

To serve, pour the gazpacho into 18 (2-ounce) shot or cordial glasses. Alternatively, pour some of the gazpacho into 6 small glasses and offer refills. Drain the pickled cucumbers and top each shooter with a small sprinkling of them.

Fruit of the Vine Burgers *with California Relish*

Diane Sparrow of Osage, Iowa, traveled to Napa Valley to participate in Sutter Home Winery's Build a Better Burger Cook-Offs in both 2001 and 2006. This wine-country burger was her creation in the first contest. Tomato preserves or jam are available in some supermarkets and from numerous mail-order sources. **Serves 6**

Relish

1 cup golden raisins
1/4 cup Sutter Home Zinfandel
1/4 cup grapeseed oil or olive oil
1/2 cup oil-packed sun-dried tomatoes
1 small red onion, cut into chunks
2 teaspoons kosher or coarse sea salt
4 small chipotle chiles in adobo sauce
6 tablespoons tomato preserves or jam

Patties

12 bottled brine-packed grape leaves, tough stems discarded
1 pound lean ground beef
1 pound lean ground pork
1 cup chopped seedless black grapes
6 tablespoons Sutter Home Zinfandel
1 1/2 teaspoons kosher or coarse sea salt
1 1/2 teaspoons crushed dried green peppercorns
3/4 cup (about 3 ounces) crumbled feta cheese

2 (1 pound) loaves artisan country-style bread, preferably roasted garlic or herb flavor, sliced 1/2 inch thick to make 12 slices
12 crisp lettuce leaves

Prepare a medium-hot fire in a charcoal grill with a cover, or preheat a gas grill to medium high.

To make the relish, combine all the ingredients in a food processor and pulse until chopped coarsely. Transfer to a bowl, cover, and refrigerate until assembling the burgers.

To make the patties, roll the grape leaves, cut the rolls into very thin strips, chop finely, and transfer to a large bowl. Add the beef, pork, grapes, wine, salt, peppercorns, and cheese. Handling the meat as little as possible to avoid compacting it, mix well. Form the mixture into 6 equal patties to fit the bread slices.

Brush the grill rack with vegetable oil. Place the patties on the rack, cover, and cook, turning once, until done to preference, about 5 minutes on each side for medium. During the last few minutes of cooking, place the bread slices on the outer edges of the rack, turning once, to toast lightly.

To assemble the burgers, on 6 of the bread slices, place 2 lettuce leaves, a patty, and a generous amount of the relish. Top with the remaining bread slices and serve.

Bibb Lettuce and Endive Salad

with Crisp Prosciutto, Pear, Goat Cheese, and Verjus

Subtly sweet leaves of Bibb, Boston, or other butterhead lettuce teams with slightly bitter spears of endive in this garden-fresh mixture dressed with *verjus* (see sidebar). **Serves 6**

Dressing

1/4 cup verjus
2 teaspoons Dijon mustard
1 teaspoon minced shallot
1 teaspoon minced fresh thyme
1 teaspoon minced fresh flat-leaf parsley
1/4 teaspoon kosher or coarse sea salt
1/8 teaspoon freshly ground black pepper
3 tablespoons walnut oil

2 heads Bibb lettuce
1 head Belgian endive, preferably red variety
9 thin slices prosciutto
1 ripe but firm pear
3/4 cup (about 3 ounces) crumbled fresh
  goat cheese

To make the dressing, combine the *verjus*, mustard, shallot, thyme, parsley, salt, and pepper in a small bowl and whisk to blend well. Add the oil and whisk until emulsified. Taste and add more salt and pepper, if desired. Cover and refrigerate until serving; whisk again, if necessary.

Remove any damaged outer leaves from the lettuce and tear the remaining leaves into 2- to 3-inch pieces. Cut off the root end of the endive and separate into individual spears. Wash the lettuce and endive in cold water and spin dry. Lay out on paper toweling or an absorbent kitchen towel and roll to wrap up. Refrigerate until well chilled.

Preheat the oven to 350°F. Line a baking sheet with parchment paper or a silicone baking mat.

Lay the prosciutto in a single layer on the baking sheet. Bake, turning once, until browned and crisp, 5 to 15 minutes, depending on the thickness of the slices. Carefully remove the prosciutto to a paper towel to cool, and then break into 2- to 3-inch pieces.

Core the pear. Cut it into thin lengthwise slices.

Combine the lettuce, endive, and pear in a serving bowl. Add just enough of the dressing to coat the leaves and toss. Add the prosciutto and half of the cheese and gently toss again, being careful not to break the delicate prosciutto. Taste and add more salt and pepper, if needed. Sprinkle on the remaining cheese and serve.

> *Verjus* is the tart, unfermented juice from wine grapes; if you can't locate it in your markets, substitute 2 tablespoons Champagne vinegar or another mild white vinegar, and increase the oil in the dressing to 6 tablespoons.

Summer Pearl Couscous Salad

Pearl couscous, also sold as Israeli or Middle Eastern couscous, is a small round pasta that is about the size of peas when cooked. **Serves 6**

2 cups pearl couscous

1/4 cup finely grated lemon zest

1/2 cup freshly squeezed lemon juice

3 tablespoons Champagne vinegar or unseasoned rice vinegar

3 tablespoons extra-virgin olive oil

1 teaspoon kosher or coarse sea salt

1 1/2 cups diced (about pea size) seeded English cucumber

6 tablespoons diced (about pea size) red onion

1 1/2 cups fresh sweet corn kernels

4 teaspoons minced garlic

2 tablespoons finely chopped fresh mint

2 tablespoons finely chopped fresh flat-leaf parsley

1 1/2 cups halved Sungold, Sweet 100, or other flavorful cherry tomatoes

Bring a large pot of salted water to a boil. Add the couscous, and cook, stirring frequently, just until al dente, about 10 minutes. Drain, rinse with cold water to cool, and drain again well.

Combine the couscous, lemon zest, lemon juice, vinegar, oil, and salt in a large stainless-steel or other nonreactive bowl, and toss to blend thoroughly. Stir in the cucumber, onion, corn, garlic, mint, and parsley. Gently fold in the tomatoes. Taste and add more lemon juice and salt, if desired. Transfer to a serving bowl and serve at room temperature.

Almond–Olive Oil Cake *with Strawberries*

This moist and not-too-sweet cake served with a spoonful of fresh berries makes a perfect ending to a wine-country meal. Packaged ground almonds (often labeled almond meal) are available in many health food stores and specialty supermarkets such as Trader Joe's and Whole Foods. You can also grind whole almonds in a food processor; use raw almonds (not blanched or roasted) and pulse a little bit at a time just until they are the texture of cornmeal, being careful not to overprocess into almond butter. **Serves 6**

Cake
1 1/2 cups ground almonds
3/4 cup all-purpose flour
1 teaspoon baking powder
1/2 teaspoon salt
1 cup sugar
3/4 cup extra-virgin olive oil
1/2 cup light cream or half-and-half, at room temperature
5 eggs, at room temperature
2 tablespoons finely grated fresh orange zest
1 teaspoon pure almond extract

3 cups sliced fresh strawberries
1 tablespoon granulated sugar
Confectioners' sugar, for dusting the cake

To make the cake, preheat the oven to 325°F. Grease a nonstick 8-inch round cake pan with cooking spray, preferably olive oil spray.

Combine the almonds, flour, baking powder, and salt in a bowl and whisk to mix well. Set aside.

Combine the sugar, oil, cream, eggs, orange zest, and almond extract in the bowl of an electric mixer. Using the paddle attachment, beat on medium speed until smooth, about 3 minutes. Add the almond–flour mixture and mix on low speed until blended.

Scrape the batter into the cake pan. Bake until a skewer inserted into the center of the cake comes out clean, about 40 minutes. Let cool in the pan on a wire rack for 10 minutes, then invert the cake onto a plate and lift off the pan. Invert the cake again onto a serving plate, top side up.

Combine the strawberries and granulated sugar in a bowl, and toss gently; taste and add a little more sugar if needed. Set aside for a few minutes to draw out the berry juices.

Using a sifter or a fine-mesh strainer, dust the top of the cake with the confectioners' sugar. Transfer the berries to a serving bowl. Cut the cake into wedges and serve with the berries.

Big Fat Greek Night
Feast of Olympian Flavors

Perfect for a "girl's night" or for any gathering of fun-loving friends, this salute to Greece combines flavorful food, exuberant music, and a delightful movie.

"Opa!" This Greek expression of delight is used much like a shout of "Hooray!" Highlighted by the prizewinning Opa! Burgers, this menu captures the sun-drenched flavors of Greece in dishes that are big, bold, and bountiful enough to make your guests shout for joy.

Look to the bright blue and white of the Greek flag for table-setting and decor inspiration. Create a cheerful table of blue-and-white-patterned linens, white dishes, and lots of white and blue votives. Big containers of seasonal Mediterranean fruits such as grapes, lemons, oranges, and pomegranates make a perfect centerpiece, perhaps with branches of olive or bay trees to complete the Grecian theme. Or line the center of the table with a row of colorful pots of bright geraniums or herbs.

Play lively Greek music to welcome guests and set the festive mood. Arrange comfortable seating in front of the TV, and, after dining, top off the evening with a Greek-themed movie such as *Mamma Mia!, Never on Sunday, Summer Lovers,* or *Zorba the Greek.*

MENU

Fava *with Pita Crisps*

Lettuce Wraps *with Warm Halloumi and Roasted Grapes*

Sutter Home Chardonnay
Sutter Home Pinot Grigio

Opa! Burgers

Grilled Eggplant *with Minted Greek Yogurt and Grilled-Tomato Sauce*

Sutter Home Merlot

Lemon–Honey Yogurt Squares

Sutter Home Moscato

Fava *with Pita Crisps*

The Greek dish known as *fava* has been a perennial favorite since the early days of that civilization. *Fava* was originally made with the broad bean from which it takes its name, but through the centuries the fava beans were replaced with yellow lentils or split peas, which are much easier to prepare. **Serves 6**

Fava

1 pound yellow split peas
1 cup chopped yellow onion
3 cloves garlic
1/2 cup extra-virgin olive oil
3 tablespoons tahini (sesame seed paste)
1 1/2 teaspoons kosher or coarse sea salt

Pita Crisps

3 pita breads, about 6 inches in diameter
1 tablespoon sesame oil
1 tablespoon vegetable oil
2 tablespoons sesame seed
1 1/2 teaspoons cumin seed
1 teaspoon kosher or coarse sea salt

1 tablespoon finely chopped fresh Greek oregano, or 1 teaspoon dried oregano
1 teaspoon finely chopped fresh thyme
6 pitted kalamata olives, finely chopped
1/2 lemon
Extra-virgin olive oil, for drizzling

To make the *fava*, spread the peas out on a flat surface and carefully pick them over to remove any imperfect ones or foreign bits. Put the peas in a colander and rinse well with cold water to remove the dust accumulated during drying and storing. Transfer to a saucepan, add the onion and 2 of the cloves of garlic, and barely cover the peas with water. Bring to a boil over medium-high heat and then decrease the heat to maintain a simmer. Cook until very tender, 45 minutes to 1 hour, adding just enough water as necessary to keep barely covered. Remove from the heat and let cool in the pan.

While the peas are cooking, finely chop the remaining garlic clove and combine it with the oil in a small saucepan. Cook over low heat just until the garlic is golden brown, about 10 minutes; watch carefully to keep the garlic from overbrowning. Strain into a small bowl through a fine-mesh strainer; save the garlic to garnish the *fava*.

Add the garlic oil, tahini, and salt to the pea mixture. Puree until smooth with an immersion blender, in a food processor, or in a standing blender. Taste and add more salt, if desired. Transfer to a bowl, cover, and refrigerate until chilled.

To make the crisps, preheat the oven to 350°F. With the tip of a knife, carefully split and separate each pita horizontally into 2 rounds. Combine the sesame oil and vegetable oil in a small bowl and brush all over the smooth side of each pita round. Sprinkle with the sesame seed, cumin seed, and salt. Cut each pita into 8 wedges, place on a baking sheet, and bake until lightly browned and crisp, about 10 minutes. Set the baking sheet on a wire rack and let cool completely.

To serve, transfer the *fava* to a shallow serving bowl and place the strained garlic in the center. Sprinkle with the oregano, thyme, and olives. Squeeze lemon juice over the top and then drizzle on a little olive oil. Surround the *fava* with the crisps.

Lettuce Wraps *with Warm Halloumi and Roasted Grapes*

Halloumi, the traditional cheese of Cyprus, holds its shape when heated. Instruct guests to wrap the cool lettuce cups around the warm cheese and eat the packets out of their hands. **Serves 6**

3 tablespoons sherry vinegar

1 teaspoon sugar

12 ounces seedless red grapes, stemmed

1 teaspoon finely grated fresh lemon zest

Pinch of kosher or coarse sea salt

Pinch of freshly ground black pepper

12 inner leaves of tender head lettuce, 4 to 5 inches in diameter, washed, dried, and chilled

8 ounces halloumi cheese, sliced into 12 (1/4-inch-thick) pieces

1/4 cup coarsely chopped toasted walnuts

3 tablespoons chiffonade-cut fresh basil leaves

Preheat the oven to 450°F.

Combine the vinegar with the sugar in a small bowl and stir to dissolve the sugar. Spread the grapes in a baking pan, pour the vinegar mixture over them, and stir to coat. Roast the grapes, stirring occasionally, until most of them are shriveled and the liquid is thick and concentrated, 25 to 30 minutes. Carefully transfer the grapes to a bowl, add the lemon zest, salt, and pepper, and gently toss.

Arrange the lettuce leaves, edges curling up, on a serving platter.

Heat a large nonstick skillet over medium-high heat. When hot, add the cheese slices and cook until speckled brown on the bottom, about 30 seconds. Turn with a spatula and cook until speckled brown on the other side, about 30 seconds.

To serve, place a slice of warm cheese in the center of each lettuce leaf. Spoon an equal portion of the roasted grapes onto each piece of cheese and then sprinkle with the walnuts and basil.

Opa! Burgers

After tasting this burger, chef Cat Cora of *Iron Chef America*, a noted Greek cooking authority and a judge for Sutter Home Winery's Build a Better Burger 2006, shouted, "Opa! This takes me back to the old country!" The other judges were equally enthusiastic and awarded creator Elizabeth Bennett of Mill Creek, Washington, the top prize for Best Alternative Burger. *Sopressata*, a dry-cured Italian sausage, is available in Italian markets or the deli section of many well-stocked supermarkets. Substitute a flavorful salami if you can't locate it. **Serves 6**

1/2 cup mayonnaise
1/4 cup chopped roasted red bell pepper
2 cups (about 8 ounces) crumbled goat feta cheese
1/2 cup pitted and chopped kalamata olives

Patties
1 cup Sutter Home Merlot
1/2 ounce dried porcini mushrooms
2 pounds ground lamb
1 tablespoon minced garlic
1/2 teaspoon dried oregano
1/4 teaspoon crushed red chile flakes
2 teaspoons salt
1/2 teaspoon freshly ground black pepper

6 Italian-style bolo rolls or other rustic rolls, split horizontally
12 thin slices sopressata
1 cup loosely packed baby spinach leaves
6 large tomato slices

Prepare a medium-hot fire in a charcoal grill with a cover, or preheat a gas grill to medium high.

Combine the mayonnaise and bell pepper in a small bowl and mix well. Cover and refrigerate until assembling the burgers.

In a separate small bowl, mash the feta with a fork. Stir in the olives; set aside.

To make the patties, pour the wine into a heavy fireproof saucepan and heat on the grill until the wine begins to simmer. Remove from the heat and add the dried mushrooms, stirring with a fork to moisten all the mushrooms. Set them aside to reconstitute for at least 30 minutes. Then drain and squeeze them gently to remove excess liquid. Chop the mushrooms and transfer to a large bowl. Add the lamb, garlic, oregano, chile flakes, salt, and pepper. Handling the meat as little as possible to avoid compacting it, mix well. Form the mixture into 6 equal patties to fit the rolls.

Brush the grill rack with vegetable oil. Place the patties on the rack, cover, and cook, turning once, until done to preference, about 4 minutes on each side for medium-rare. During the last few minutes of cooking, place the rolls, cut side down, on the outer edges of the rack to toast lightly.

To assemble the burgers, spread the mayonnaise mixture over the cut sides of the roll bottoms and the feta mixture over the cut sides of the roll tops. On each roll bottom, place a patty, 2 slices of the *sopressata*, some spinach leaves, and a tomato slice. Add the roll tops and serve.

Grilled Eggplant *with Minted Greek Yogurt and Grilled-Tomato Sauce*

Choose any variety, shape, or color of eggplant when making this flavor-packed side dish.

Serves 6

Minted Yogurt

2 cups plain Greek-style yogurt

1 teaspoon finely grated fresh lemon zest

1 tablespoon freshly squeezed lemon juice

2 teaspoons finely chopped garlic

1/4 cup chopped fresh mint

1 tablespoon chopped fresh Greek oregano, or 1 teaspoon dried oregano

1 teaspoon kosher or coarse sea salt

1/4 teaspoon freshly ground black pepper

1/2 teaspoon cumin seed

Grilled Eggplant

2 pounds eggplant

1/2 cup extra-virgin olive oil

2 teaspoons finely grated fresh lemon zest

3 tablespoons freshly squeezed lemon juice

1 teaspoon finely chopped garlic

1 tablespoon finely chopped fresh thyme

Tomato Sauce

6 vine-ripened red heirloom tomatoes

2 tablespoons extra-virgin olive oil, plus more for brushing

2 teaspoons finely chopped garlic

1/4 cup finely chopped fresh basil

1 teaspoon kosher or coarse sea salt

Pinch of ground allspice

Kosher or coarse sea salt, for sprinkling

To make the minted yogurt, combine the yogurt, lemon zest, lemon juice, garlic, mint, oregano, salt, and pepper in a bowl and mix well. Taste and add more lemon juice, salt, and pepper, if desired. Cover and refrigerate for at least 1 hour.

Put the cumin seed in a small skillet and toast over medium heat, shaking the pan frequently, until fragrant, 1 to 2 minutes. Pour onto a plate to cool, then transfer to a spice grinder, and grind until fine. Set aside until serving.

To prepare the grilled eggplant, slice each eggplant into 1/2-inch-thick slices and place in a large glass baking dish. Combine the oil, lemon zest, lemon juice, garlic, and thyme in a small bowl and whisk to blend. Pour evenly over the eggplant and immediately turn the slices to coat. Let marinate for 30 minutes.

Prepare a medium fire in a charcoal grill with a cover, or preheat a gas grill to medium.

To make the tomato sauce, coat the tomatoes lightly with the brushing oil. Place on the grill rack, cover, and cook, turning occasionally, until partially charred and slightly softened, 3 to 5 minutes. Transfer to a food processor and pulse until chopped yet still chunky. Remove to a serving bowl and stir in the 2 tablespoons oil and the garlic, basil, salt, and allspice.

Sprinkle the marinated eggplant with salt to taste. Place on the grill rack, cover, and cook, turning once, until well browned and tender, 3 to 5 minutes per side. Remove to a serving platter.

Stir the chilled yogurt sauce well and sprinkle with the cumin. To serve, offer the minted yogurt and tomato sauces alongside the eggplant.

Lemon-Honey Yogurt Squares

This simple cake soaks up the honey-lemon syrup while cooling in its pan. If you can locate goat milk yogurt, use it for even more tang. **Serves 6**

Syrup
1/2 cup honey
1/2 cup water
2 tablespoons shredded fresh lemon zest
2 tablespoons freshly squeezed lemon juice

Cake
1 1/4 cups all-purpose flour
1/4 teaspoon baking powder
1/4 teaspoon baking soda
1/4 teaspoon salt
1/4 cup (1/2 stick) unsalted butter, at room
   temperature
1 cup sugar
2 tablespoons finely grated fresh lemon zest
2 eggs, at room temperature
1/2 teaspoon pure lemon extract
3/4 cup plain yogurt (not fat free), at room
   temperature
1/2 cup sliced almonds, lightly toasted

To make the syrup, combine the honey and water in a small saucepan. Bring to a boil over medium-high heat, then decrease the heat to maintain a simmer, stir in the lemon zest, and cook, stirring occasionally, until the consistency of a thin syrup, about 10 minutes. Stir in the lemon juice and set aside to cool to room temperature.

To make the cake, preheat the oven to 350°F. Butter an 8-inch square cake pan.

Combine the flour, baking powder, baking soda, and salt in a bowl and whisk to mix well.

Combine the butter, sugar, and lemon zest in the bowl of an electric mixer. With the paddle attachment, beat on medium speed for about 5 minutes. Add the eggs and beat well. Add the lemon extract and blend well. On low speed, add about one-third of the flour mixture and then half of the yogurt, mixing just until the ingredients are incorporated. Then add half of the remaining flour mixture, followed by the remaining yogurt, and finally the remaining flour mixture.

Scrape the batter into the buttered pan. Bake until a skewer inserted into the center of the cake comes out clean, 30 to 35 minutes. Remove the pan to a wire rack and pierce the cake top with a skewer at 1-inch intervals all over. Strain the cooled syrup into a small pitcher or liquid measuring cup, reserving the lemon zest, and pour the syrup evenly over the top of the cake. Let cool completely.

To serve, cut the cake into small squares in the pan and transfer to a serving platter. Arrange the almonds and reserved lemon zest over the squares.

Burgers and Blues
New Orleans Jazz Brunch

Mention New Orleans and most folks conjure up images of fabulous food, great jazz, and Mardi Gras.

Fabulous food is guaranteed with our menu of dishes that capture the authentic flavors of New Orleans and the surrounding bayou country. The Big Easy is known as a drinking city, so we've included our version of one of its famed cocktails to get everyone in the party spirit. On the other hand, don't forget to offer café au lait, a mix of strong coffee—preferably a New Orleans brand laced with chicory—and plenty of hot milk.

Some legendary New Orleans–style jazz establishes the right ambience for this leisurely and lively party; consider recordings of Louis Armstrong, Al Hirt, the Preservation Hall Jazz Band, the Neville Brothers, and Harry Connick Jr.

Elements of Mardi Gras can be brought into play with the table setting. Party stores offer an array of bead necklaces in the carnival colors of purple, green, and gold, and strewing piles of these trinkets on the table can't be beat. While searching for beads, look for masks and other Mardi Gras decorations, too.

If you decide to throw this party during Mardi Gras season (the several weeks preceding Lent, after Fat Tuesday), greet your guests with traditional beads and masks. Or ask them to arrive in colorful costumes. Tell them to come prepared to *"laissez les bons temps rouler"* (let the good times roll), as they say in Southern Louisiana.

MENU

Hurricanes

Bluesiana Burgers with Zydeco Sauce, Mardi Gras Slaw, and Root Beer Glaze

Red Beans and Rice Salad with Tabasco Vinaigrette

Shrimp Remoulade Potato Salad

Sutter Home Chardonnay
Sutter Home Zinfandel

Bananas Foster Upside-Down Cake

Sutter Home Moscato

Café au Lait

Hurricane

Legendary New Orleans bar owner Pat O'Brien gets credit for creating the original Hurricane during the 1940s. Our version adds fruity White Zinfandel to the mix in place of some of the traditional spirits. The glasses, shaped like globes of hurricane lamps, are essential for capturing the essence of the drink; they're readily available from numerous online shopping sites. The drinks should be made one at a time, so the proportions are listed for a single serving. **Serves 1**

Crushed ice or ice cubes
3 ounces Sutter Home White Zinfandel
1 1/2 ounces dark rum
1 1/2 ounces almond liqueur
1 1/2 ounces passion fruit or guava juice
1 1/2 ounces freshly squeezed orange juice
3/4 ounce pomegranate juice
3/4 ounce freshly squeezed lemon juice

Garnish
1 fresh orange slice
1 fresh lemon slice
1 maraschino cherry

Add crushed ice or ice cubes to half-fill a 15-ounce hurricane glass. Combine all the drink ingredients in a shaker with a handful of ice and shake vigorously. Strain into the glass, garnish with the fruit slices and cherry, and serve.

Bluesiana Burgers *with Zydeco Sauce, Mardi Gras Slaw, and Root Beer Glaze*

The 2008 Sutter Home Winery's Build a Better Burger competition called for entries that represented the contestant's hometown, state, or region of the country. First runner-up George Graham from Lafayette, Louisiana, described his homage to South Louisiana as "A dash of mystery. A pinch of history. If you want to learn the language of Cajun food, you have to immerse yourself in the Louisiana culture. It is our rich heritage of extraordinary cooking, foot-stomping music, and fun-filled Mardi Gras that inspired this unique burger. It's spicy, saucy, crunchy, colorful, exotic, hypnotic, and dripping with the rhythm of a bayou beat."

Root beer extract is readily available in some parts of the country, as well as from online grocers. If you can't locate it, pour a cup of root beer into a small saucepan and cook over medium-high heat until reduced to a thick syrup. **Serves 6**

Sauce
1 cup mayonnaise
2 tablespoons prepared horseradish
1 tablespoon Worcestershire sauce
1 tablespoon whole-grain mustard
1 tablespoon Tabasco pepper sauce
1 teaspoon crushed red chile flakes

Glaze
1 1/2 cups root beer soda
1 cup bottled chili sauce
1/4 cup freshly squeezed lemon juice
3 tablespoons Worcestershire sauce
1 1/2 tablespoons dark brown sugar
1 tablespoon dark molasses
1 teaspoon liquid smoke

1 teaspoon root beer extract
1/2 teaspoon ground ginger
1/2 teaspoon garlic powder
1/2 teaspoon onion powder
1/4 teaspoon kosher or coarse sea salt
1/4 teaspoon freshly ground black pepper

Slaw
1 1/2 cups thinly shredded green cabbage
1/4 cup thinly shredded purple cabbage
1/4 cup very thinly sliced red onion
1/4 cup thinly sliced fennel bulb
1/4 cup very thinly sliced yellow bell pepper
2 tablespoons sugar cane vinegar or distilled white vinegar
1 1/2 teaspoons whole-grain mustard
1/2 teaspoon kosher or coarse sea salt
1/2 teaspoon freshly ground black pepper
1/4 cup extra-virgin olive oil
1/2 cup (about 2 ounces) finely crumbled mild blue cheese

Patties
2 pounds ground chuck
1 tablespoon Tabasco pepper sauce
1/4 cup finely chopped green onions, including green tops
2 teaspoons kosher or coarse sea salt
2 teaspoons freshly ground black pepper

1/2 cup (1 stick) butter, melted
6 high-quality hamburger buns, split

continued

Bluesiana Burgers, *continued*

Prepare a medium-hot fire in a charcoal grill with a cover, or preheat a gas grill to medium high.

To make the sauce, combine all the ingredients in a bowl and mix well. Cover and refrigerate until assembling the burgers.

To make the glaze, combine all the ingredients in a heavy fireproof saucepan. Cook on the grill, stirring occasionally, until the glaze is reduced to about 1 cup and thick enough to coat the back of a spoon, 10 to 15 minutes. Taste and add more salt and pepper, if desired. Remove $1/3$ cup of the glaze and reserve until assembling the burgers. Set aside the rest of the glaze until cooking the patties (the sauce will thicken slightly as it cools).

To make the slaw, combine the green and purple cabbages, onion, fennel, and bell pepper in a bowl. In another bowl, combine the vinegar, mustard, salt, and pepper and whisk to blend well. Add the oil and whisk until emulsified. Pour the dressing over the slaw mixture and toss.

Add the cheese and toss again, evenly distributing the cheese. Cover and refrigerate until assembling the burgers.

To make the patties, combine all the ingredients in a large bowl. Handling the meat as little as possible to avoid compacting it, mix well. Form the mixture into 6 equal patties to fit the buns.

Brush the grill rack with vegetable oil. Place the patties on the rack, cover, and cook, turning once and brushing with the glaze, until done to preference, about 5 minutes on each side for medium. During the last few minutes of cooking, brush the melted butter on the cut sides of the buns and place them, cut side down, on the outer edges of the rack to toast lightly.

To assemble the burgers, spread a generous amount of the sauce over the cut sides of the buns. On each bun bottom, place a patty, and brush again with the reserved glaze. Drain off excess liquid from the slaw and place a portion on each patty. Add the bun tops and serve.

Red Beans and Rice Salad *with Tabasco Vinaigrette*

The beloved red beans and rice of New Orleans team up in a new guise as a flavorful salad. The zesty dressing features Louisiana's favorite elixir, Tabasco, which is made on Avery Island near the burger creator's hometown of Lafayette. The favorite beans of South Louisiana are the small red beans; if you can't find them canned, substitute 3 cups of cooked dried ones or canned red kidney beans. Creole mustard, a spicy blend of brown whole-grain mustard with horseradish, is available in specialty food markets and the gourmet section of many supermarkets. If you can't locate it, blend two parts brown whole-grain mustard with one part prepared horseradish.

Serves 6

Vinaigrette
1/4 cup white wine vinegar
1 tablespoon Creole mustard
2 teaspoons Tabasco pepper sauce
1 1/2 teaspoons minced or pressed garlic
1 teaspoon kosher or coarse sea salt
1/2 cup extra-virgin olive oil

2 (15-ounce) cans small red beans, drained and rinsed
3 cups cooked long-grain white rice, at room temperature
1/2 cup diced (1/4 inch) red bell pepper
1/2 cup diced (1/4 inch) green bell pepper
1/2 cup diced (1/4 inch) celery
1/2 cup very thinly sliced green onions, including green tops
1/4 cup diced (1/4 inch) carrot
1/4 cup finely chopped fresh flat-leaf parsley

To make the vinaigrette, combine the vinegar, mustard, pepper sauce, garlic, and salt in a small bowl and whisk to blend well. Add the oil and whisk until emulsified. Taste and add more pepper sauce and salt, if desired.

Shortly before serving, combine the beans, rice, bell peppers, celery, green onions, carrot, and parsley in a large bowl. Add the vinaigrette and toss to coat.

To serve, transfer the salad to a serving platter or bowl.

Shrimp Remoulade Potato Salad

Shrimp remoulade is a very popular dish in New Orleans, appearing often on brunch menus. We've teamed it with potatoes for a hearty side dish that complements the zesty burgers.

Serves 6

Remoulade

1 cup mayonnaise

1/4 cup Dijon mustard

2 tablespoons ketchup

2 teaspoons prepared horseradish

1 1/2 teaspoons Tabasco pepper sauce

1 teaspoon Worcestershire sauce

2 tablespoons freshly squeezed lemon juice

1 tablespoon sweet paprika

1 teaspoon kosher or coarse sea salt

2 1/2 pounds russet or large Yukon Gold potatoes, peeled and cut into 3/4-inch chunks

2 teaspoons salt

1 pound cooked bay shrimp or other small salad shrimp

3/4 cup sliced celery

1/2 cup sliced green onions, including green tops

1/4 cup finely chopped fresh flat-leaf parsley

To make the remoulade, combine all the ingredients in a small bowl and whisk to blend well. Cover and refrigerate until ready to use.

Put the potatoes and salt in a pot and add cold water to cover. Bring to a boil over medium-high heat, decrease the heat to maintain a simmer, and cook just until the potatoes are tender when pierced with a skewer or fork, about 10 minutes. Drain and set aside to cool slightly.

Combine the warm potatoes with the shrimp, celery, green onions, and parsley in a large bowl. Add enough of the dressing to coat, and toss; refrigerate the remaining dressing for serving. Cover and refrigerate the salad until chilled.

To serve, toss with more of the dressing, if desired, and transfer to a serving bowl.

Bananas Foster Upside-Down Cake

The rich New Orleans dessert of flambéed bananas served with vanilla ice cream was created at the world-famous Brennan's restaurant in the French Quarter to honor a friend of the owner's. For decades it has been a favorite way for New Orleanians and visitors alike to end a hearty breakfast at the legendary restaurant and has been imitated everywhere. Here we use the banana preparation to top an upside-down cake, another southern classic. **Serves 6**

3/4 cup (1 1/2 sticks) unsalted butter, at room temperature
1/2 cup firmly packed dark brown sugar
1/4 cup dark rum
3/4 teaspoon ground cinnamon
About 2 1/2 cups sliced (1/4 inch, crosswise) ripe but firm bananas
1 1/2 cups all-purpose flour
1 1/2 teaspoons baking powder
1/2 teaspoon salt
3/4 cup granulated sugar
2 eggs, at room temperature
1 teaspoon pure vanilla extract
1/2 cup milk (not nonfat), at room temperature
Premium vanilla ice cream, for serving

Preheat the oven to 350°F. Butter a 9-inch round cake pan.

Combine 1/4 cup of the butter with the brown sugar, rum, and cinnamon in a saucepan. Cook over medium heat, stirring frequently, until the butter and sugar are melted, about 3 minutes.

Pour into the cake pan. Arrange enough banana slices to fit very snugly in one layer over the butter mixture; the bananas will shrink during baking.

Combine the flour, baking powder, and salt in a bowl and whisk to mix well.

Combine the remaining 1/2 cup butter and the granulated sugar in the bowl of an electric mixer. With the paddle attachment, beat on medium speed until very light and fluffy, about 5 minutes. Add the eggs and beat well. Add the vanilla and blend well. On low speed, add about one-third of the flour mixture and then half of the milk, mixing just until the ingredients are incorporated. Then add half of the remaining flour mixture, followed by the remaining milk, and finally the remaining flour mixture. Scrape the batter into the pan and carefully spread it evenly over the fruit.

Bake until a skewer inserted into the center of the cake comes out clean, about 40 minutes. Let cool in the pan on a wire rack for about 2 minutes. Then, run a paring knife around the inside of the pan to loosen the cake sides, invert the cake onto a wide serving plate, and lift off the pan; the sauce will run down the sides of the cake onto the plate. If any fruit sticks to the pan, remove it with a spatula and reposition it on the cake.

Cut into wedges and serve warm (reheat briefly in a microwave oven, if necessary) with scoops of ice cream.

Burgers in Paradise
Tropical Patio Party

Everyone craves a bit of the aloha spirit of Hawaii from time to time. We created this party as a summer gathering on the patio, but you may choose to adapt it to the indoors during the bleakest winter days to warm your friends with tropical feeling. In either case, decorate the space and table with tropical fabrics, flowers, foliage, and seashells.

Don't forget to encourage guests to wear aloha shirts or muumuus when you issue the invitations. Plan to greet guests at the door with flower leis, preferably real ones, now available from many mainland florists or shipped from online Hawaii stores, or buy good fake leis from a party store or website.

An endless array of recorded Hawaiian music is available from past and current artists to add the right note. Some of our favorites include Andy Cummings and His Hawaiian Serenaders, Kahauanu Lake Trio, The Maikai Gents with the Mysterious Miss Mauna Loa, Na Palapalai, Ku'uipo Kumukahi, Hapa, and Keali'i Reichel. You might have a friend or two who plays ukulele or dances hula, so invite them to share their talents.

If the party is planned to last into the evening, place some tiki torches around the patio or lawn for a dramatic effect.

MENU

Vintner's Vacations

Grilled Maui Onion Dip *with Taro Chips*

Hawaii Da Kine Burgers *with Sweet Chili Glaze, Ginger-Goat Cheese Spread, and Hot Watercress Salad*

Island Rice Salad *with Ginger-Citrus Dressing*

Sutter Home Sauvignon Blanc
Sutter Home White Merlot

Haupia Pudding

Macadamia Sandies

Sutter Home Moscato

Vintner's Vacation

Napa Valley Chardonnay takes a Hawaiian holiday and makes a big splash in this Polynesian punch. Cream of coconut, a highly sweetened coconut product, can be found among the mixers in liquor stores and supermarkets. The amounts provided below are for a single serving, because the drinks need to be made one at a time. **Serves 1**

4 ounces Sutter Home Chardonnay

2 ounces almond liqueur

2 ounces pineapple juice

1 ounce freshly squeezed pomelo or grape-fruit juice

1 ounce freshly squeezed lime juice

1 ounce cream of coconut, preferably Coco Lopez brand

Ice cubes or crushed ice

1 fresh pineapple slice, for garnish

Combine the wine, liqueur, juices, and cream of coconut in a cocktail shaker with a handful of ice. Shake vigorously, then strain into a tall glass and add ice, if desired. Garnish with a pineapple slice and serve.

Grilled Maui Onion Dip *with Taro Chips*

Salty chips and a sweet onion dip are a good counterpoint to sweet tropical drinks. If you can't locate taro roots or prefer not to fry your own, look for commercial taro chips in many upscale supermarkets, or substitute Hawaiian-style potato chips. **Serves 6**

Dip

1 Maui or other sweet onion, peeled and cut into 1/2-inch slices (kept intact)

Olive oil, for brushing and drizzling

4 cloves garlic, peeled

1 cup sour cream

1/2 cup mayonnaise

2 teaspoons finely grated fresh lime zest

2 teaspoons finely chopped fresh flat-leaf parsley

1/2 teaspoon kosher or coarse sea salt

1/4 teaspoon ground cayenne

1/4 teaspoon ground white pepper

Chips

Peanut oil, for frying

3 large taro roots, about 2 inches in diameter, peeled

Popcorn salt or other fine salt, for sprinkling

To make the dip, prepare a medium fire in a charcoal grill with a cover, or preheat a gas grill to medium. Brush the onion slices on both sides with some of the oil. Put the garlic cloves in the middle of a 6-inch square of aluminum foil and drizzle with oil. Bring up the sides of the foil and seal. Place the onion slices and foil packet on the grill rack, cover, and cook, turning the onion slices once, until the slices are nicely browned, 3 to 4 minutes per side. Transfer the slices and the garlic packet to a cutting board. Open the foil and let both onion and garlic cool to room temperature.

Combine the sour cream, mayonnaise, lime zest, parsley, salt, cayenne, and pepper in a bowl and blend thoroughly. Finely chop the onion and garlic and stir into the sour cream mixture. Taste and add more salt, cayenne, and pepper, if desired. Cover and refrigerate until well chilled.

To make the chips, pour 2 inches of oil into a deep fryer or saucepan and heat to 325°F.

Using a mandoline or a very sharp knife, slice the taro about 1/16-inch thick. Place as many slices as will fit in a single layer into the hot oil and fry, turning occasionally, until crisp and lightly browned, about 2 minutes. Remove to paper towels to drain and, while still hot, sprinkle with salt to taste. Repeat until all the chips are done.

To serve, transfer the dip to a serving bowl and surround with the chips on a plate or tray.

Hawaii Da Kine Burgers *with Sweet Chili Glaze, Ginger–Goat Cheese Spread, and Hot Watercress Salad*

Kristine Snyder, a harpist from Kihei, Hawaii, in 2008 won both the Grand Prize and the People's Choice Award at Sutter Home Winery's Build a Better Burger contest with this island-inspired burger. She had also won the Grand Prize in 2001 with her Soy-Glazed Salmon Burgers. Months before her second BBB victory, she'd won the Food Network's Ultimate Recipe Showdown: Burgers, and in 2003 she was awarded the Grand Prize for a burger at the National Chicken Cooking Contest. All these triumphs make her arguably America's burger queen.

In explaining why her burger was a great local American burger, Kristine wrote, " 'Da kine' is a key phrase in Hawaiian Pidgin, the language of the 'locals.' It can mean almost anything, but often refers to something good or genuine, or, as in this case, 'the best.' This burger is as local as it gets, in both taste and ingredients." **Serves 6**

Cheese Spread

4 ounces garlic–chive goat cheese or other garlic-flavored mild goat cheese

1/2 cup mayonnaise

1 1/2 tablespoons finely minced fresh ginger

Glaze

2/3 cup bottled Thai sweet chili sauce

1 1/2 tablespoons Japanese soy sauce

Patties

3 ounces spicy Portuguese sausage (linguiça)

2 pounds ground chuck

1/3 cup minced ripe papaya

1/3 cup minced Maui or other sweet onion

1 1/2 tablespoons plus 1 teaspoon McCormick's Gourmet Collection Asian-Style Spiced Sea Salt, or 1 1/2 teaspoons coarse sea salt

6 high-quality seeded hamburger buns or sandwich rolls, split

Salad

3 tablespoons macadamia nut oil or peanut oil

2 small ripe Hass avocados, pitted, peeled, and thinly sliced lengthwise

1 1/2 tablespoons freshly squeezed lemon juice, preferably Meyer variety

1/2 ripe papaya, coarsely chopped

5 cups chopped fresh watercress

2 small Maui or other sweet onions, thinly sliced and separated into rings

2 1/2 teaspoons minced garlic

1/4 teaspoon crushed red chile flakes

2 tablespoons Japanese soy sauce

Prepare a medium-hot fire in a charcoal grill with a cover, or preheat a gas grill to medium high.

To make the spread, combine all the ingredients in a small bowl. Cover and refrigerate until assembling the burgers.

To make the glaze, combine all the ingredients in a small bowl. Set aside.

To make the patties, process the sausage in a food processor until finely chopped. Transfer to a large bowl and add the chuck, papaya, onion, and spiced salt. Handling the meat as little as possible to avoid compacting it, mix well. Form the mixture into 6 equal patties to fit the buns.

continued

Brush the grill rack with vegetable oil. Place the patties on the rack, cover, and cook, turning once and basting often with the glaze, until done to preference, about 5 minutes on each side for medium. During the last few minutes of cooking, place the buns, cut side down, on the outer edges of the rack to toast lightly. Cover the patties and buns with aluminum foil to keep warm while preparing the salad.

To make the salad, pour the oil into a fireproof skillet and heat on the grill until it reaches its smoking point. While the oil is heating, halve the avocado slices and place in a large bowl. Add the lemon juice and toss gently. Layer the papaya, watercress, onions, garlic, and chile flakes over the avocado and carefully drizzle the hot oil over the top. Add the soy sauce and toss to combine.

To assemble the burgers, spread the cheese spread over the cut sides of the bun tops. On each bun bottom, place a patty, and top with the salad. Add the bun tops and serve.

Island Rice Salad *with Ginger-Citrus Dressing*

Jeffrey's flavor-packed salad captures the essence of contemporary Hawaiian cuisine and pairs perfectly with the burgers. **Serves 6**

Dressing
1/4 cup freshly squeezed orange juice
2 tablespoons unseasoned rice vinegar
2 tablespoons soy sauce
1 tablespoon Dijon mustard
1 tablespoon light brown sugar
1 tablespoon minced fresh ginger
1 tablespoon minced garlic
1/4 teaspoon kosher or coarse sea salt
1/4 teaspoon freshly ground black pepper
1/4 cup Asian sesame oil
1/4 cup peanut oil

4 cups cooked long-grain white rice
3/4 cup finely diced mango
1/4 cup finely diced red bell pepper
1/2 cup chopped green onions, including green tops
1/4 cup chopped fresh cilantro
1/4 cup chopped roasted macadamia nuts

To make the dressing, combine the orange juice, vinegar, soy sauce, mustard, sugar, ginger, garlic, salt, and pepper in a small bowl and whisk to blend well. Add the oils and whisk until emulsified. Taste and add more salt, if desired.

Shortly before serving, combine the rice, mango, bell pepper, green onions, cilantro, and macadamia nuts in a large bowl. Add the dressing and toss to coat.

To serve, transfer the salad to a serving platter or bowl.

Haupia Pudding

In Hawaii, a luau often ends with squares of *haupia*, a stiffened coconut milk dessert. This softer, creamier "pudding" version showcases the clean taste of lightly sweetened pure coconut. Not all canned coconut milks are created equal, so choose a high-quality brand; our favorite is Chaokoh from Thailand. Crisp Macadamia Sandies (page 48) are the perfect partner to the velvety smooth coconut. **Serves 6**

$^1/_2$ cup sugar
$^1/_4$ cup cornstarch
2 (13.5-ounce) cans coconut milk
Pesticide-free small orchids, for garnish (optional)

Combine the sugar and cornstarch in a heavy saucepan. Gradually whisk in the coconut milk until the mixture is smooth. Cook over medium heat, whisking constantly, until the mixture just comes to a boil and thickens slightly, about 5 minutes.

Divide the pudding into 6 (4-ounce) serving bowls, let cool to room temperature, and then cover and refrigerate until completely chilled, at least 2 hours.

To serve, garnish each pudding with an orchid.

Macadamia Sandies

Although rich and buttery, these delicate cookies are as soft on the palate as the white sands of Maui beaches are on the feet. **Serves 6**

- 3/4 cup (1 1/2 sticks) unsalted butter, at room temperature
- 6 tablespoons sugar
- 1/8 teaspoon salt
- 1 teaspoon pure vanilla extract
- 1 1/2 cups all-purpose flour
- 1 cup finely chopped roasted unsalted macadamia nuts

Place the butter in the bowl of an electric mixer. With the paddle attachment, beat at medium speed until soft and creamy, about 45 seconds. Add the sugar and salt and mix until well blended. Add the vanilla and blend well. Add the flour and mix at low speed until the dough is smooth, about 2 minutes. Add the nuts and mix until thoroughly incorporated. Scrape the dough onto a sheet of parchment paper or plastic wrap. Using a ruler as a guide, form the dough into an even, flat rectangle about 8 by 3 inches. Bring the paper or plastic wrap up around the dough to enclose it, and refrigerate until firm, at least 2 hours.

Preheat the oven to 350°F. Line 2 baking sheets with parchment paper or silicone baking mats.

Unwrap the dough. Slice it along a shorter side into 1/4-inch-thick slices, and place them about 1 inch apart on one of the baking sheets until the sheet is full. (Rewrap and refrigerate the remaining dough to keep it firm while baking the first batch of sandies.) Bake until the tops of the slices are pale golden all over, about 15 minutes; the edges will be lightly browned, but do not allow the tops to brown. Slide the paper or mat off the baking sheet to a wire rack to cool completely. Repeat the slicing, baking, and cooling with the remaining dough on the other baking sheet. (Depending on the size of your baking sheets, you may need to repeat with a third batch of sandies; let the baking sheet cool completely and wipe away any crumbs from the paper or mat before reusing it.)

By the Sea
Picnic at the Shore

Pack up a portable grill and head to the seaside, or at least to a nearby body of water, for a relaxing afternoon. Before you go, check with beach authorities about using a grill. Throw in a folding table and chairs to make seaside dining more comfortable and keep sand out of the food. You may wish to include a Frisbee, volleyball, or other game for fun in the sand. Don't forget the sunscreen and beach towels!

Prepare the food, including the burger patties, at home, and refrigerate in well-sealed containers. Just before leaving home, transfer the food containers to a cooler with plenty of ice.

Enjoy the deviled eggs and lemonade while the fish patties are sizzling, and then dig into the tasty burgers with sides of crunchy slaw and one of the best potato salads you'll ever eat. Round out the seaside repast with a chunky chocolate cookie or two.

Leave the music player at home and enjoy the natural rhythm of the sea in harmony with the sounds of nature.

MENU

Spanish Deviled Eggs (Huevos Diablos)

Fresh Lemonade

Ocean State Swordfish Burgers *with Tangy Apple Tartar Sauce*

Roasted Fingerling Potato Salad *with Basil Vinaigrette*

Fennel and Jicama Slaw *with Citrus Dressing*

Sutter Home Chardonnay
Sutter Home Sauvignon Blanc
Sutter Home White Zinfandel

Cherry-Chocolate Chunk Cookies

Spanish Deviled Eggs (Huevos Diablos)

Ideally, start with eggs about 10 days old, because fresher eggs are more difficult to peel after cooking. The recipe includes two extra eggs in case of breakage.

Piquillo, Spanish for "little beak," describes the shape of the small, pimento-type sweet peppers grown in northern Spain. They are roasted over an open fire to enhance their flavor before they are packed. Look for them and smoked paprika in upscale supermarkets and specialty food stores. If you can't find Spanish chorizo, use a similar garlic-flavored sausage like Portuguese linguiça. **Serves 6**

14 eggs
1 teaspoon freshly squeezed lemon juice
$1/8$ teaspoon Spanish saffron
$1/2$ cup mayonnaise
2 teaspoons Dijon mustard
1 ounce firm fully-cooked Spanish chorizo, finely chopped
Pinch of ground cayenne
Kosher or coarse sea salt
Freshly ground black pepper

Salsa
3 piquillo peppers, patted dry and finely chopped
1 teaspoon smoked sweet paprika (pimentón dulce)
1 tablespoon finely chopped fresh chives
1 teaspoon minced garlic
1 teaspoon olive oil
Kosher or coarse sea salt

The day before cooking the eggs, turn them on their sides in their carton, to allow the yolks to center in the whites, and refrigerate; you won't be able to close the carton lid.

About an hour before cooking, remove the eggs from the refrigerator, to help prevent cracking during cooking.

Place the eggs in a single layer in the bottom of a large saucepan and cover with cold water. Cover the pot and bring just to a boil over medium-high heat. Remove the pan from the heat and let stand, covered, for 15 minutes. Prepare a large bowl of iced water. Carefully remove the eggs from the pan with a large slotted spoon and

set them in the bowl of iced water until cold. To peel, tap each egg on a work surface until finely cracked all over. Gently roll each egg on the surface to loosen the shells and return the egg to the iced water (the water will get under the shell and aid in peeling). Peel off the shells, rinse the eggs to remove any shell bits, and refrigerate the eggs for at least 30 minutes.

Add the lemon juice to the saffron in a small bowl to soften it.

Slice the eggs in half lengthwise and pop the yolks into a bowl. With the back of a fork, mash the yolks until finely crumbled. Add the mayon- naise, mustard, lemon–saffron mixture, chorizo, and cayenne. Season to taste with salt and pepper and thoroughly blend. Scrape the yolk mixture into a pastry bag or a sealable plastic bag with a bottom corner snipped off, and pipe the mixture into the egg white halves. Alternatively, spoon the yolk mixture into the whites. Cover and refriger- ate until just before serving.

To make the salsa, combine all the ingredients, including salt to taste, in a bowl, and mix well.

To serve, arrange the eggs on an egg dish or serving plate and top each with a small dollop of the salsa.

Fresh Lemonade

Is there anything better than old-fashioned lemonade for cooling off on a hot summer afternoon? If you're familiar with only frozen or packaged varieties, then meet the real thing. What a difference!

Use superfine sugar, sold alongside regular sugar, because its fine granules dissolve quickly in liquid. Depending on the tastes of your group, you may wish to double or triple this recipe.

Serves 6

2 quarts cold water
2 cups freshly squeezed lemon juice (from about 18 lemons)
1 1/2 cups superfine sugar
Ice cubes, for serving
Lemon slices, for serving

Combine the water, lemon juice, and sugar in a large pitcher, and stir until the sugar dissolves.

To serve, place ice cubes in glasses and add lemonade and lemon slices.

Ocean State Swordfish Burgers
with *Tangy Apple Tartar Sauce*

"With almost 400 miles of tidal coastline in Rhode Island, one does not have to go far to find superb seafood," wrote Wakefield resident Valerie Szlatenyi of her 2008 Alternative Burgers People's Choice winning recipe in Sutter Home Winery's Build a Better Burger competition. "One of the local favorites is fresh swordfish, which is abundant in the summer and fall. This swordfish burger with the popular Portuguese sweet roll is a great way to enjoy the wonderful fresh ocean taste, making it a perfect local American burger, especially when paired with Sutter Home Chardonnay. You will feel like you are on vacation! Any freshly baked soft roll can be substituted for the Portuguese sweet roll; however, the sweetness of the Portuguese roll complements the fish, adding another dimension to the overall flavor." **Serves 6**

Tartar Sauce
1/2 cup mayonnaise
1/3 cup chopped bread-and-butter pickles
1/3 cup chopped tart apple
1 teaspoon McCormick Old Bay Seasoning
1/2 teaspoon freshly squeezed lemon juice

Patties
1 1/2 pounds swordfish meat, finely chopped
1/2 cup panko (Japanese bread crumbs)
1/4 cup crushed cornflakes
1/4 cup chopped bread-and-butter pickles
1/4 cup minced sweet onion

1 egg, lightly beaten
1 tablespoon minced garlic
1/2 teaspoon finely chopped fresh dill
5 teaspoons McCormick Old Bay Seasoning
1/4 teaspoon salt
1/4 teaspoon freshly ground black pepper

6 Portuguese sweet rolls, split
2 cups shredded crisp lettuce

Prepare a medium-hot fire in a charcoal grill with a cover, or preheat a gas grill to medium high.

To make the sauce, combine all the ingredients in a bowl and stir to blend thoroughly. Cover and refrigerate until assembling the burgers.

To make the patties, combine all the ingredients in a large bowl and mix gently. Form the mixture into 6 equal patties to fit the rolls.

Brush the grill rack with vegetable oil. Place the patties on the rack, cover, and cook, turning once, just until opaque throughout, about 4 minutes on each side. During the last few minutes of cooking, place the rolls, cut side down, on the outer edges of the rack to toast lightly.

To assemble the burgers, on each roll bottom, place an equal amount of lettuce, a patty, and an equal amount of the tartar sauce. Add the roll tops and serve.

Roasted Fingerling Potato Salad *with Basil Vinaigrette*

We just can't get enough potato salad alongside burgers, and here's a mayonnaise-free version destined to become a crowd-pleaser. **Serves 6**

Vinaigrette

1/4 cup champagne vinegar

3 tablespoons minced fresh basil

2 tablespoons Dijon mustard

1 tablespoon minced garlic

2 anchovy filets, minced

1/2 teaspoon kosher or coarse sea salt

1/4 teaspoon freshly ground black pepper

1/2 cup extra-virgin olive oil

3 pounds fingerling potatoes (about 1 inch in diameter)

3 tablespoons olive oil

Kosher or coarse sea salt, for sprinkling

Freshly ground black pepper, for sprinkling

1/2 cup chopped oil-packed sun-dried tomatoes

1/2 cup pitted and halved kalamata olives

1/2 cup chopped green onions, including green tops

1/4 cup (about 1 ounce) coarsely grated Asiago cheese

1 cup croutons (about 1/2-inch cubes)

To make the vinaigrette, combine the vinegar, basil, mustard, garlic, anchovies, salt, and pepper in a small bowl and whisk to blend well. Add the oil and whisk until emulsified. Taste and add more salt and pepper, if desired.

Preheat the oven to 350°F.

Slice the potatoes in half lengthwise and place in a bowl. Add the oil, sprinkle with salt and pepper to taste, and toss to coat well. Transfer to a large baking pan or rimmed baking sheet and roast, stirring occasionally, until tender when pierced with a knife or skewer, 30 to 40 minutes. Let the potatoes cool in the pan, and then transfer to a large bowl. Add the tomatoes, olives, green onions, and cheese and stir gently to combine. Add the vinaigrette and gently toss the salad. Taste and add more salt and pepper, if desired. Cover and refrigerate until chilled.

To serve, gently stir in the croutons and transfer to a serving bowl.

Fennel and Jicama Slaw *with Citrus Dressing*

This crunchy salad with citrus dressing pairs perfectly with the swordfish burgers. A mandoline slicer makes quick work of prepping the vegetables; use the regular slicing blade at the thinnest position for the fennel, and then insert the julienne blade for the jicama. **Serves 6**

2 bulbs fennel with fronds
1 small jicama (about 1 pound), peeled and cut into julienne (about 6 cups)
1/2 cup sliced (1 inch long) fresh chives
1/2 cup freshly squeezed orange juice
1/4 cup orange liqueur
1/4 cup extra-virgin olive oil
1 tablespoon freshly squeezed lime juice
1/2 teaspoon crushed red chile flakes
Kosher or coarse sea salt
Freshly ground black pepper

Remove the fronds from the fennel and chop enough fronds to yield 1/4 cup. Core the fennel bulbs and slice very thinly. Transfer to a serving bowl along with the chopped fronds. Add all the remaining ingredients, including salt and pepper to taste, and toss to mix well. Cover and refrigerate for 1 hour. Toss again just before serving.

Cherry–Chocolate Chunk Cookies

Who doesn't love a good chocolate chip cookie? These large cookies, featuring big chunks of chocolate instead of chips, are all about the quality of the chocolate—and the cherries. Be sure to buy bars that you'd enjoy eating on their own. Intensely flavored dried tart or sour cherries, such as the Montmorency variety, make a perfect partner to the dark chocolate; use small cherries whole or chop larger ones. **Serves 6**

1 1/4 cups all-purpose flour

1/2 teaspoon baking soda

1/2 teaspoon salt

1/2 cup (1 stick) unsalted butter, at room temperature

1/2 cup granulated sugar

1/2 cup firmly packed light brown sugar

1 egg, at room temperature

2 teaspoons pure vanilla extract

12 ounces premium dark chocolate bars (about 70% cacao), coarsely chopped into 1/2-inch pieces

1 cup pitted dried tart cherries

Preheat the oven to 350°F. Line 2 baking sheets with parchment paper or silicone baking mats.

In a bowl, combine the flour, baking soda, and salt. Whisk to mix well.

Combine the butter and both sugars in the bowl of an electric mixer. With the paddle attachment, beat at medium speed until the mixture is light and fluffy, about 5 minutes. Add the egg and vanilla and blend well. Add the flour mixture and mix at low speed just until incorporated. Stir in the chopped chocolate and cherries.

Using a #20 (1/4-cup) ice-cream scoop with a release mechanism, scoop up level portions of the dough and place them about 3 inches apart on one of the baking sheets. (Cover the bowl with the remaining dough to keep it from drying out while the first batch of cookies bakes.) Bake until the cookies are golden brown, about 15 minutes. Slide the paper or mat off the baking sheet to a wire rack to cool completely. Repeat the forming, baking, and cooling process with the remaining dough on the other baking sheet.

Fall Frolic
Autumn Harvest Afternoon

Crisp autumn air somehow makes good food taste even better. Our menu starts with a wine cocktail spiced with apple juice and almond liqueur. Then we move on to smoky bacon burgers topped with a crunchy apple and blue cheese slaw. Potato salad with roasted green chiles and pumpkin seed, a platter of grilled autumn fruits drizzled with a tangerine-flavored yogurt, and a warm salad of green beans are perfect accompaniments. To end the fall feast, we offer a rich variation on an American classic.

Decorate the party area with pumpkins, gourds, apples, cornstalks, Indian corn, and fall leaves. Select tableware in earthy shades of gold, orange, rust, and brown, which look great on an uncovered wood table. We chose a country barn for this party, scattered straw on the floor, and added bales of straw for casual seating.

Country music fits the mood of this party, and you may wish to play an array of styles from bluegrass to rockabilly.

Before serving dessert, guide the group on a brisk walk to enjoy the countryside or a nearby park.

MENU

Applause Cocktails

Smoky-Sweet Bacon Burgers
with Apple-Blue Cheese Slaw

Green Chile-Potato Salad
with Roasted Pumpkin Seeds

Grilled Autumn Fruits
with Tangerine-Yogurt Dressing

Warm Baby Green Bean Salad
*with Applewood Bacon and
Sherry Vinaigrette*

**Sutter Home Sauvignon Blanc
Sutter Home Chardonnay
Sutter Home Merlot**

Butterscotch Pecan Pie
with Bourbon Whipped Cream

Sutter Home Moscato

Applause Cocktail

Greet guests with an apple-based cocktail to provide a hint of the apple-topped burgers to come. These shaken drinks are best made one at a time, so amounts are listed for single servings. **Serves 1**

1 apple wedge, about 1/4 inch thick, cored
4 ounces Sutter Home Chardonnay
2 ounces apple juice
1/2 ounce almond liqueur
1/2 ounce orange liqueur
1/2 ounce anise liqueur
Ice cubes

Put the apple wedge in a small tumbler. Combine the remaining ingredients in a cocktail shaker with some ice and shake for 30 seconds. Strain the mixture over the apple wedge and serve.

Smoky-Sweet Bacon Burgers *with Apple-Blue Cheese Slaw*

Jamie Miller of Maple Grove, Minnesota, received the Grand Prize at the 2000 Sutter Home Winery's Build a Better Burger Cook-Off with her Tuna Burgers with Maui Wowee Salsa, and she returned in 2008 as a finalist with this recipe shortly after winning the top prize in Rachel Ray's burger contest and being a runner-up to her friend Kristine Snyder (page 45) in Food Network's Ultimate Recipe Showdown. **Serves 6**

Slaw

3 large Granny Smith apples, peeled, cored, and grated

2 teaspoons finely grated fresh lemon zest

2 1/2 tablespoons freshly squeezed lemon juice

1/3 cup mayonnaise

2 tablespoons pure maple syrup

2 celery stalks, very thinly sliced

1 cup (about 4 ounces) crumbled firm blue cheese, preferably Maytag from Iowa or St. Pete's from Minnesota

1/3 cup minced fresh chives

1/2 teaspoon sweet paprika

1/4 teaspoon freshly grated nutmeg

12 slices thick-cut applewood-smoked bacon

Patties

1/2 cup grated red onion

1/4 cup Sutter Home Sauvignon Blanc

1/3 cup minced fresh flat-leaf parsley

2 tablespoons Worcestershire sauce

3 tablespoons pure maple syrup

2 tablespoons minced fresh thyme

1 1/2 teaspoons kosher or coarse sea salt

1 teaspoon freshly ground black pepper

3/4 teaspoon ground cumin

3/4 teaspoon smoked paprika

1/2 teaspoon ground cayenne

1/4 teaspoon ground allspice

2 pounds ground chuck

6 Kaiser rolls, split

6 large leafy lettuce leaves

Prepare a medium-hot fire in a charcoal grill with a cover, or preheat a gas grill to medium high.

To make the slaw, gently squeeze the apples between layers of paper towels to remove some of the excess moisture. Place the apples in a large bowl, add the lemon zest and juice, and toss to coat. Stir in the mayonnaise, maple syrup, celery, cheese, chives, paprika, and nutmeg. Cover and refrigerate until assembling the burgers.

In a fireproof skillet, cook the bacon on the grill until crisp. Transfer to paper towels to drain and wrap in aluminum foil to keep warm.

To make the patties, combine the onion, wine, parsley, Worcestershire sauce, maple syrup, thyme, salt, pepper, cumin, paprika, cayenne, and allspice in a large bowl and whisk together. Add the beef, and, handling the meat as little as possible to avoid compacting it, mix well. Form the mixture into 6 equal patties to fit the rolls.

Brush the grill rack with vegetable oil. Place the patties on the rack, cover, and cook, turning once, until done to preference, about 5 minutes on each side for medium. During the last few minutes of cooking, place the rolls, cut side down, on the outer edges of the rack to toast lightly.

To assemble the burgers, on each roll bottom, place a lettuce leaf, a patty, 2 slices of bacon, and a serving of slaw. Add the roll tops and serve.

Green Chile–Potato Salad *with Roasted Pumpkin Seeds*

Roasted New Mexican green chiles are used in the dressing and also tossed into this southwestern-inspired salad; Jeffrey prefers chiles from the area around Hatch, New Mexico. Look for *crema* in the refrigerated sections of many major supermarkets or in Latin markets. **Serves 6**

Dressing

1 teaspoon whole cumin seed

4 ounces fresh green New Mexico chiles, roasted, peeled, seeded, and chopped, or 1 (4-ounce) can diced green chiles, drained

3/4 cup mayonnaise

3/4 cup crema (Mexican sour cream) or sour cream

2 tablespoons apple cider vinegar

1 tablespoon juice from canned or pickled jalapeño chiles

1 teaspoon kosher or coarse sea salt

1/4 teaspoon freshly ground black pepper

3 pounds small red potatoes (about 1 1/2 inches in diameter), preferably Red Bliss variety

1 tablespoon salt

4 ounces fresh green New Mexico chiles, roasted, peeled, seeded, and chopped, or 1 (4-ounce) can diced green chiles, drained

1/2 cup chopped green onions, including green tops

1/2 cup chopped fresh cilantro

1 cup roasted and salted shelled pumpkin seed (pepitas)

To make the dressing, toast the cumin seed in a small skillet over medium heat, shaking the pan frequently, until fragrant, 1 to 2 minutes. Pour onto a plate to cool, then transfer to a spice grinder and grind until fine. Combine the remaining dressing ingredients with the cumin in a food processor or blender and blend until smooth. Taste and add more salt and pepper, if desired. Transfer to a bowl, cover, and refrigerate until ready to use.

Put the potatoes and salt in a pot and add cold water to cover. Bring to a boil over medium-high heat. Decrease the heat to maintain a simmer and cook just until the potatoes are tender when pierced with a skewer or fork, about 15 minutes. Drain and let cool slightly. Halve or quarter each warm potato and transfer to a large bowl. Add enough of the dressing to coat and toss; refrigerate the remaining dressing for serving. Add the chiles and toss again. Cover and refrigerate until chilled.

To serve, add the green onions, cilantro, 3/4 cup of the pumpkin seed, and more of the dressing, if desired, and toss. Transfer to a serving bowl or platter and sprinkle with the remaining pumpkin seed.

Grilled Autumn Fruits *with Tangerine-Yogurt Dressing*

Crisp Fuyu persimmon slices would be another nice addition to this display of seasonal fruits.

Serves 6

Dressing

1 cup freshly squeezed tangerine juice
1 tablespoon honey
1 cup plain whole-milk yogurt

2 firm, crisp apples
2 firm, crisp pears
6 firm, ripe figs
2 tablespoons olive oil
1 teaspoon finely chopped fresh thyme
Kosher or coarse sea salt, for sprinkling
Freshly ground black pepper, for sprinkling
1/4 cup pomegranate seeds
1/4 cup chiffonade-cut fresh mint leaves

To make the dressing, pour the tangerine juice into a small saucepan and bring to a simmer over medium heat, then adjust the heat to maintain the simmer and cook until reduced to 1/2 cup, 15 to 20 minutes; use a heatproof measuring cup to check the quantity. Remove from the heat, add the honey, and stir until dissolved. Taste and add more honey, if desired. Let cool completely, and then combine with the yogurt in a small serving bowl. Cover and refrigerate until serving.

Prepare a low to medium fire in a charcoal grill with a cover, or preheat a gas grill to medium low.

Core each apple and pear and slice into 8 wedges. Halve the figs lengthwise. Combine the fruit, olive oil, and thyme in a bowl, sprinkle to taste with salt and pepper, and gently toss to coat. Place the fruit on the grill rack, cover, and cook, turning once, just until marked and heated through but still slightly firm, about 1 minute per side; do not overcook.

To serve, arrange the grilled fruits on a serving platter and scatter the pomegranate seeds and mint over the top. Offer the dressing alongside for drizzling over the fruits.

Warm Baby Green Bean Salad *with Applewood Bacon and Sherry Vinaigrette*

Yes, we know that there's already bacon on the burgers, but we don't think you can ever have too much of a good thing! If you can't find dry Jack cheese, substitute Parmesan or Asiago. **Serves 6**

> $1/4$ pound sliced applewood-smoked bacon, cut crosswise into $1/8$-inch strips
>
> $1 1/2$ pounds young, tender green beans (haricots verts), trimmed
>
> 1 roasted red bell pepper, peeled, seeded, and sliced lengthwise into $1/4$-inch strips
>
> $1/4$ cup toasted pine nuts

Vinaigrette

> 3 tablespoons sherry vinegar
>
> 1 tablespoon Dijon mustard
>
> 2 teaspoons honey
>
> 3 tablespoons minced shallot
>
> 1 tablespoon bacon fat
>
> 2 tablespoons walnut oil

> Kosher or coarse sea salt, for sprinkling
>
> Freshly ground black pepper, for sprinkling
>
> 2 ounces dry Jack cheese, shaved with a vegetable peeler

Cook the bacon in a large sauté pan over medium heat until browned and crisp. Remove with a slotted spoon to paper towels to drain. Set aside 1 tablespoon of the bacon fat in the pan for later use and discard the rest.

Bring a large pot of heavily salted water to a boil. Add the green beans and cook just until crisp-tender, about 5 minutes. Drain and transfer to a large bowl. Add the bell pepper and 3 tablespoons of the pine nuts and toss to combine.

To make the vinaigrette, combine the vinegar, mustard, honey, and shallot in a small bowl and mix well. Return the pan with the bacon fat to medium heat, add the walnut oil, and bring just to a simmer. Add the vinegar mixture and cook, whisking to blend, for about 1 minute.

To serve, pour the warm vinaigrette over the beans and toss well. Sprinkle with salt and pepper to taste. Transfer to a warmed serving platter and scatter the bacon, cheese, and remaining pine nuts over the beans.

Butterscotch Pecan Pie *with Bourbon Whipped Cream*

For big time-savers, look for packaged pecans that are already toasted and chopped, and use a commercial pie crust. Boxed crusts that you unfold and place in a pie pan are available in the refrigerator sections of most supermarkets, as are frozen crusts already formed in disposable pans (be sure to measure that they really are 9 inches in diameter, or the filling will not all fit). For best baking results, we recommend using a 9-inch glass pie pan; if using a commercial formed crust, remove it from the disposable pan while still frozen, place it in the glass pan, let it thaw, and press it into the pan to fit. A pie crust shield, available in good cookware stores, is a helpful and inexpensive investment for any baker. **Serves 6**

Pie
- 1/2 cup firmly packed light brown sugar
- 1 tablespoon all-purpose flour
- 1/4 teaspoon salt
- 1 cup light corn syrup
- 1/4 cup (1/2 stick) unsalted butter, melted and cooled slightly
- 1 teaspoon pure vanilla extract
- 3 eggs, at room temperature
- 2 cups (about 8 ounces) chopped toasted pecans
- 1 cup butterscotch chips
- 1 unbaked 9-inch pie crust, thawed if frozen

Whipped Cream
- 1 cup heavy whipping cream, well chilled
- 2 tablespoons confectioners' sugar
- 1 tablespoon bourbon

Preheat the oven to 375°F.

To make the pie, combine the brown sugar, flour, salt, corn syrup, butter, vanilla, and eggs in a bowl and whisk until well blended. Stir in the pecans and butterscotch chips and pour into the pie crust. Cover the rim of the crust with a long strip of aluminum foil or a pie crust shield, to prevent overbrowning during baking. Bake until the edges of the pie feel set when touched but the center still wobbles slightly, about 50 minutes; the filling should remain just a bit gooey but not syrupy, and a knife inserted into the center should still have tracings of filling when removed.

Set the pie plate on a wire rack to cool.

To make the whipped cream, just before serving, pour the cream into a bowl and beat with a whisk or an electric mixer just until the cream begins to thicken. Add the confectioners' sugar and bourbon and continue to beat just until the cream holds its shape softly; be very careful not to overbeat if using an electric mixer.

Serve the pie warm or at room temperature with the whipped cream.

Festa Italiana
Italy in Your Backyard

Italian feasts are held throughout the year to honor numerous saints and special occasions, and all are bountiful with great food and wine. Create your own *festa* by setting a backyard table in the official colors of Italy, with white plates and alternating green and red napkins. Create an edible centerpiece with clusters of fresh red and green table grapes.

Streamers or banners of green, red, and white tied to trees, poles, or an arbor can add to the festivities. If you choose to host the party in the evening, stretch strings of globe lights (available from party light websites) over the dining area.

Welcome your guests with our riff on the Venetian Bellini cocktail and a classic antipasto of roasted peppers with fresh mozzarella. Warm potatoes and a grilled radicchio salad complement the sausage burgers. Chilled zabaglione, made with Italian lemon liqueur instead of the traditional Marsala, ends the *festa* on a light note.

Play famous Neapolitan songs or opera arias sung by Caruso, Pavarotti, or Bocelli. Or listen to the soundtrack from the movie *Big Night* or some Dean Martin Italian pop. For a special occasion, hire a local Italian accordionist to play at the party.

MENU

Chardonnay Bellinis

Roasted Bell Peppers
with Buffalo Mozzarella

Little Italy Sausage Burgers

Crisp New Potatoes
with White Truffle Oil and Parmigiano-Reggiano

Grilled Radicchio Salad
with Pear, Walnuts, Gorgonzola, and Balsamic Vinaigrette

Sutter Home Zinfandel
Sutter Home Red

Chilled Limoncello Zabaglione

Sutter Home Moscato

Chardonnay Bellinis

A combination of Chardonnay and lemon-lime soda stands in for the traditional sparkling wine in our version of Venice's famed Bellini. **Serves 6**

1 1/2 cups peeled and chopped white peaches
1/4 cup chopped raspberries
8 ounces Sutter Home Chardonnay
2 ounces peach nectar
1 tablespoon apricot preserves
Lemon-lime soda, chilled

Combine the peaches, raspberries, wine, peach nectar, and preserves in a bowl and refrigerate until thoroughly chilled, about 2 hours. Shortly before serving, transfer to a blender and blend until smooth.

To serve, pour the peach mixture into 6 champagne flutes, filling them two-thirds full, and then top with the soda.

Roasted Bell Peppers *with Buffalo Mozzarella*

This simple dish is all about the finest quality ingredients. *Mozzarella di bufala* is made from the rich milk of water buffalo that live in marshlands outside of Naples. To ensure freshness, purchase it from a cheese shop that receives frequent air shipments from Italy. If you absolutely can't locate the authentic import, use the finest and freshest cow's milk mozzarella available.

This is the time to break out your best bottle of olive oil. And dress up the dish with capers, balsamic vinegar, white anchovies, or other Italian ingredients that strike your fancy. Be creative!
Serves 6

4 or 5 bell peppers, any combination of red, yellow, and orange, with straight, smooth sides
1 pound fresh mozzarella di bufala cheese
20 fresh basil leaves
Fruity extra-virgin olive oil, for drizzling
Kosher or coarse sea salt, for sprinkling
Freshly ground black pepper, for sprinkling

Place the peppers directly over a gas flame or on a baking sheet under a broiler. Roast, turning with tongs as needed, until the skins are charred and blackened all over; the timing will depend on the intensity and proximity of the heat. Transfer to a bowl, cover tightly with plastic wrap or aluminum foil, and let steam for about 2 minutes. Using your fingertips or a paring knife, rub or scrape away the charred skin; do not rinse. Cut off the tops, slit each pepper lengthwise, and open flat. Trim the ragged edges and remove the inner membranes and seeds with a paring knife. Tear or cut the peppers into 2- or 3-inch pieces.

With a very sharp knife, slice the cheese into 1/4-inch slices.

To serve, alternate the peppers, cheese, and basil attractively on a serving platter. Drizzle with olive oil and sprinkle with salt and pepper to taste.

Little Italy Sausage Burgers

Henderson, Nevada, resident Rebecca Reese loves Italian sausage, and her experiment in making a burger with its familiar flavors won her the prize in 2007 for Best Alternative Burger at Sutter Home Winery's Build a Better Burger contest.
Serves 6

2/3 cup mayonnaise
1/3 cup bottled red wine vinaigrette

Patties
1 pound bulk sweet Italian sausage
1 pound ground pork
1/2 cup chopped pickled pepperoncini
1/2 cup (about 2 ounces) grated Asiago cheese
1/2 cup Italian-style bread crumbs
1 1/2 teaspoons kosher or coarse sea salt
1/4 teaspoon freshly ground black pepper

9 ounces fresh mozzarella cheese, cut into 6 equal slices
6 bun-sized pieces focaccia bread, sliced horizontally, or focaccia buns, split
6 thin slices red onion
2 cups coarsely shredded romaine lettuce

Prepare a medium-hot fire in a charcoal grill with a cover, or preheat a gas grill to medium high.

Combine the mayonnaise and vinaigrette in a small bowl and mix well. Cover and refrigerate until assembling the burgers.

To make the patties, combine all the ingredients in a large bowl. Handling the meat as little as possible to avoid compacting it, mix well. Form the mixture into 6 equal patties to fit the bread pieces.

Brush the grill rack with vegetable oil. Place the patties on the rack, cover, and cook, turning once, until done to preference, about 4 minutes on each side for medium. During the last few minutes of cooking, place the cheese slices on the patties to melt and place the bread pieces, cut side down, on the outer edges of the rack to toast lightly.

To assemble the burgers, spread the mayonnaise mixture on the cut sides of each bread piece. On each bread bottom, place a patty, an onion slice, and a portion of the lettuce. Add the bread tops and serve.

Crisp New Potatoes *with White Truffle Oil and Parmigiano-Reggiano*

The classic Italian flavors of white truffles and nutty Parmesan cheese enhance warm roasted potatoes in this side dish, which pairs perfectly with the sausage burgers. **Serves 6**

2 pounds small (about 1 inch in diameter) new potatoes

2 tablespoons olive oil

Kosher or coarse sea salt

1 1/2 tablespoons white truffle oil

1 cup (about 4 ounces) finely grated Parmigiano-Reggiano cheese

1/4 cup sliced (1/2 inch in length) fresh chives

1/2 teaspoon ground white pepper

Preheat the oven to 450°F.

Slice the potatoes in half lengthwise and place in a large bowl. Add the olive oil, sprinkle lightly with salt, and toss to coat the potatoes. Transfer to a roasting pan and spread in a single layer. Roast, turning occasionally, until tender and browned on all sides, 20 to 25 minutes.

Transfer the hot potatoes to a large bowl. Add the truffle oil, cheese, chives, and pepper and mix gently. Taste and add more salt, if desired.

Transfer to a serving dish and serve warm.

Grilled Radicchio Salad *with Pear, Walnuts, Gorgonzola,*
and Balsamic Vinaigrette

Grilling mellows the bitterness of the radicchio in this unusual salad, which includes pear chunks, toasted walnuts, and Gorgonzola cheese.

Serves 6

3 large firm heads radicchio
Olive oil, for brushing
Kosher or coarse sea salt, for sprinkling
Freshly ground black pepper, for sprinkling

Vinaigrette
1 tablespoon finely chopped shallot
2 teaspoons Dijon mustard
1/4 cup balsamic vinegar
1 tablespoon honey
1/2 teaspoon kosher or coarse sea salt
1/4 teaspoon freshly ground black pepper
1/2 cup extra-virgin olive oil

1 ripe but firm pear
3/4 cup (about 3 ounces) crumbled
   Gorgonzola cheese
1 cup walnut halves, toasted and coarsely
   chopped
1 tablespoon snipped chives

Prepare a medium fire in a charcoal grill with a cover, or preheat a gas grill to medium.

Cut each radicchio head into 6 wedges, leaving the cores intact to keep the leaves together. Lightly brush each wedge with oil and sprinkle lightly with salt and pepper. Place the wedges on the grill rack, cover, and cook, turning once, until lightly browned and crisp-tender, about 1 minute per side. Arrange on a serving platter and let cool to room temperature.

To make the vinaigrette, combine the shallot, mustard, vinegar, honey, salt, and pepper in a medium bowl and whisk to blend well. Add the oil and whisk until emulsified. Taste and add more salt and pepper, if desired.

To serve, drizzle the radicchio with the vinaigrette. Peel and core the pear and cut it into 1/4-inch dice. Sprinkle the pear, cheese, walnuts, and chives over the radicchio.

Chilled Limoncello Zabaglione

The delicious *limoncello* liqueur of southern Italy adds lots of lemon flavor to this chilled version of whipped zabaglione. Serve with purchased Italian amaretti cookies for a textural counterpoint to the smooth custard. **Serves 6**

6 egg yolks, at room temperature
6 tablespoons sugar
1/2 cup limoncello, at room temperature
1 cup heavy whipping cream
6 lemon slices, for garnish
Amaretti, for serving

Beat the egg yolks in a stainless-steel bowl with a whisk or an electric mixer until blended. Add the sugar and beat until pale yellow and very creamy. Gradually beat in the *limoncello* until smooth. Place the bowl over a saucepan containing barely simmering water and beat the custard until hot and thickened, about 4 minutes. Remove from the simmering water and let cool completely.

Pour the cream into a bowl and beat with a whisk or an electric mixer just until it holds its shape well; be very careful not to overbeat if using an electric mixer. Fold the whipped cream into the cooled custard, incorporating it well. Spoon the mixture equally into 6 dessert bowls or glasses. Cover tightly with plastic wrap and refrigerate until well chilled.

To serve, garnish each serving with a lemon slice. Pass a plate of amaretti at the table.

Flip 'n' Splash
Poolside Gathering

Could there be a more idyllic way to spend a perfect summer afternoon than splashing in a pool and lounging beside the water with a cocktail in hand, while enjoying the enticing aroma of burgers being flipped on the grill?

We've kept this party simple and easy. For poolside safety, bring out the colorful plastic plates and shatterproof glasses. Just add a few floats and beach balls, and perhaps a setup for a game of pool volleyball.

Add to the festivities by playing 1960s party music with a summer beat—classic Motown artists like Smokey Robinson and the Miracles, the Temptations, and the Supremes, plus other artists such as the Beach Boys, Leslie Gore, and Elvis Presley. You might even get a "pool dance" going with popular moves from that era like the Swim!

Our easy menu stars a burger packed with sunny Thai flavors and topped with crisp vegetables. For guests to nibble before the burgers are done, pick up a prepared assortment of sushi from your favorite place. To accompany the burgers, fill a big bowl with crunchy potato chips, and serve our refreshing watermelon salad. Cold, sweet ice-cream "burgers" top off the afternoon.

MENU

Sushi Platter

Sweet-Hot Thai Burgers
with Cilantro Mayonnaise and Thai Salad

Watermelon–Blue Cheese Salad

Potato Chips

Sutter Home Riesling
Sutter Home White Zinfandel
Sutter Home Red

Nutty Ice-Cream "Burgers"

Sutter Home Moscato

Sweet-Hot Thai Burgers *with Cilantro Mayonnaise and Thai Salad*

Karen Bernards's love of both Thai food and good burgers helped the resident of McMinnville, Oregon, create this recipe, which won the Sutter Home Winery's Build a Better Burger 2007 Grand Prize. The lively flavors are perfect for a poolside party. **Serves 6**

Mayonnaise
1 cup mayonnaise
1 tablespoon freshly squeezed lime juice
1/4 cup chopped fresh cilantro

Patties
2 pounds ground chuck
2 teaspoons kosher or coarse sea salt
3/4 cup bottled Thai sweet chili sauce
1/2 cup thinly sliced green onions, including green tops
1 cup crushed Spicy Thai Kettle Chips

Thai Salad
1/4 cup freshly squeezed lime juice
2 teaspoons minced garlic
1 tablespoon extra-virgin olive oil
3/4 teaspoon kosher or coarse sea salt
2 teaspoons bottled Thai sweet chili sauce
1 tablespoon grated fresh ginger
1/2 cup chopped fresh cilantro
1/4 cup chopped fresh Thai basil
1 hothouse (English) cucumber, cut into matchsticks
1 red bell pepper, cut into matchsticks
1 1/2 cups fresh bean sprouts

6 high-quality potato buns, split

Prepare a medium-hot fire in a charcoal grill with a cover, or preheat a gas grill to medium high.

To make the mayonnaise, combine all the ingredients in a small bowl and whisk to blend. Cover and refrigerate until assembling the burgers.

To make the patties, combine all the ingredients in a large bowl. Handling the meat as little as possible to avoid compacting it, mix well. Form the mixture into 6 equal patties to fit the buns.

To make the salad, combine the lime juice, garlic, oil, salt, chili sauce, ginger, cilantro, and basil in a large bowl and whisk to blend. Add the cucumber, bell pepper, and bean sprouts and toss to coat with the dressing.

Brush the grill rack with vegetable oil. Place the patties on the rack, cover, and cook, turning once, until done to preference, about 5 minutes on each side for medium. During the last few minutes of cooking, place the buns, cut side down, on the outer edges of the rack to toast lightly.

To assemble the burgers, spread a generous amount of the mayonnaise over the cut sides of the buns. On each bun bottom, place a grilled patty and a serving of the salad. Add the bun tops and serve.

Watermelon–Blue Cheese Salad

For a colorful presentation of this cooling summer salad, you may wish to alternate red and yellow watermelon slices. **Serves 6**

Dressing
3 tablespoons freshly squeezed orange juice
2 tablespoons freshly squeezed lime juice
1 tablespoon unseasoned rice vinegar
1 tablespoon honey

1 small (not baby or mini) seedless watermelon (about 10 pounds)
1/4 cup (about 1 ounce) crumbled mild blue cheese or feta cheese
1/4 cup thinly sliced red onion
1/4 cup chopped toasted pecans
3 tablespoons chiffonade-cut fresh mint leaves
Kosher or coarse sea salt, for sprinkling
Freshly ground black pepper, for sprinkling

To make the dressing, combine all the ingredients in a small bowl and whisk to blend well.

Cut the watermelon lengthwise into quarters. Cut the quarters crosswise into slices about 1 inch thick to produce 12 full-size pieces; save any remaining watermelon for another use. Cut off the rinds and arrange the slices on a large platter, creating 2 rows of 6 overlapping slices.

To serve, scatter the cheese, onion, pecans, and mint over the watermelon and drizzle with the dressing. Sprinkle with salt and pepper to taste.

Nutty Ice-Cream "Burgers"

Our version of ice-cream sandwiches, these "burgers" of rich ice cream between homemade, crumbly peanut butter cookies make an irresistible treat. Be sure to use a creamy, homogenized peanut butter, not a product that needs stirring. You may opt to use only one flavor of ice cream to fill all the cookies, or use two or three flavors for variety and extra pleasure.

The "burgers" really taste best when assembled just before serving, while the cookie "buns" are fresh (your guests might have fun building their own). Or assemble them in advance and keep them frozen until a little before serving; but be sure to let them soften a bit or the cookies will be too hard. **Serves 6**

Cookies
1 1/2 cups all-purpose flour
1/2 teaspoon baking soda
1/2 teaspoon salt
1 cup creamy, homogenized peanut butter, at room temperature
1/2 cup (1 stick) unsalted butter, at room temperature
3/4 cup granulated sugar
3/4 cup firmly packed light brown sugar
1 egg, at room temperature

3 cups premium vanilla, dulce de leche, or chocolate ice cream, softened

To make the cookies, preheat the oven to 350°F. Line 2 baking sheets with parchment paper or silicone baking mats.

In a bowl, combine the flour, baking soda, and salt and whisk to mix well.

Combine the peanut butter, butter, and sugars in the bowl of an electric mixer. With the paddle attachment, beat at medium speed until the mixture is smooth and creamy, about 5 minutes. Add the egg, and blend well. Add the flour mixture, and mix at low speed just until incorporated.

Using a #40 (2-tablespoon) ice-cream scoop, scoop up level portions of dough, roll to form balls, and place about 2 inches apart on one of the baking sheets. (Cover the bowl with the remaining dough to keep it from drying out while you bake the first batch of cookies.) Press down on the dough balls to form each ball into a round about 3/8 inch thick, and smooth the edges of each round. Bake until the cookies are lightly browned, about 12 minutes. Slide the paper or mat off the baking sheet to a wire rack to cool completely. Repeat the forming, baking, and cooling process with the remaining dough on the other baking sheet. You should have a total of about 24 cookies.

To assemble, turn half of the cookies upside down. Scoop up 1/4-cup portions of the ice cream and place on the upside-down cookies. Top with the remaining cookies, placed right side up, and press gently to sandwich the ice cream between the cookies.

Serve immediately. Or, if assembling ahead, place the "burgers" on a baking sheet, freeze until set, then transfer to freezer bags and keep frozen. Just before serving, transfer to a serving dish and let soften at room temperature for a few minutes.

From the Good Earth
Celebrating Bounty in the Garden

The spectacular produce of America's farms, orchards, and vineyards is always cause for foodies to celebrate. Berkeley, California, is arguably the birthplace of the movement to use locally produced foods in season, and our Born in Berkeley Burgers pay homage to that principle. The burgers are complemented with sides of grilled garden-fresh vegetables, crisp salad, and perfectly ripe heirloom tomatoes. Summer berries served with silky *panna cotta* round out the tribute to summer's bounty and the efforts of America's small farmers.

Choose a date at the height of the growing season and set up a table and chairs right alongside the rows of vegetables in your garden, or throw a picnic blanket on the ground for a more casual feast. The brilliant tones of Fiesta, Bauer, or other vintage pottery dishes are perfect, but any colorful dishes are at home in the garden setting. There's no better centerpiece for this theme than a basket or tray of gorgeous fresh produce from your garden or a nearby farmers' market.

Classical chamber music playing softly in the background will add to the pastoral mood of the gathering.

MENU

Melon Coolers

Born in Berkeley Burgers
(a.k.a. Bacon Cheeseburgers with Aged Teleme, Arugula-Fig Topping, Pepper Bacon, and Lemon-Grilled Fennel)

Heirloom Tomato Salad

Grilled Marinated Vegetables
with Balsamic Syrup

Sutter Home Sauvignon Blanc
Sutter Home Red
Sutter Home Zinfandel

Buttermilk Panna Cotta
with Honeyed Berries

Sutter Home Moscato

Melon Coolers

Luscious ripe melons are spiked with wine, rum, and orange liqueur in this blended drink served with muddled mint. **Serves 6**

8 cups diced ripe melons (any combination of cantaloupe, Crenshaw, honeydew, or Sharlyn)
6 ounces Sutter Home White Zinfandel
6 ounces freshly squeezed lime juice
4 ounces light rum
2 ounces Triple Sec
6 tablespoons sugar
1 cup fresh mint leaves

Combine the melons, wine, lime juice, rum, Triple Sec, and sugar in a pitcher or bowl, cover, and refrigerate until thoroughly chilled, about 2 hours.

To serve, divide the mint equally among 6 tall glasses and crush or muddle the leaves to release their essential oils. Transfer the melon mixture to a blender and blend until smooth. Pour over the mint, dividing evenly.

Born in Berkeley Burgers (a.k.a. Bacon Cheeseburgers with Aged Teleme, Arugula-Fig Topping, Pepper Bacon, and Lemon-Grilled Fennel)

College professor, fitness instructor, and cookbook author Camilla Saulsbury of Nacogdoches, Texas, wrote about her 2006 Sutter Home Winery's Build a Better Burger Grand Prize–winning burger, "I was born in Berkeley and grew up in the San Francisco East Bay. This burger captures many of my food experiences, food memories, and favorite ingredients growing up there, such as picking Meyer lemons, herbs, and tomatoes out of my parents' garden, shopping for fresh fruits and vegetables with my mom at Monterey Market, discovering and sampling all varieties of locally produced (e.g., northern California Teleme) and exotic cheeses at Berkeley's Cheese Board Cooperative, and grilling burgers with my dad in the backyard (often a teeth-chattering summertime experience, thanks to the evening fog; we would huddle around the grill for heat!). A bacon cheeseburger is the very best kind of burger in my book; this just has what I consider my own East Bay spin." **Serves 6**

Grilled Fennel

4 fennel bulbs, sliced into rings
2 tablespoons freshly squeezed lemon juice, preferably Meyer variety
2 tablespoons extra-virgin olive oil
1/4 teaspoon kosher or coarse sea salt
2 teaspoons grated fresh lemon zest, preferably Meyer variety

12 slices thick-cut pepper bacon or thick-cut regular bacon

Patties

2 pounds ground chuck
3/4 cup packed fresh basil leaves, chopped
3/4 cup chopped oil-packed sun-dried tomatoes
1/2 cup grated onion
1 tablespoon minced garlic
1 1/2 teaspoons kosher or coarse sea salt

3/4 pound aged Teleme, Brie, or Camembert cheese, sliced thinly
6 high-quality hamburger buns, split

Topping

1/2 cup chopped walnuts
4 teaspoons balsamic vinegar
1/4 cup extra-virgin olive oil
Kosher or coarse sea salt
6 fresh figs, sliced lengthwise
3 cups baby arugula, coarsely torn

Prepare a medium-hot fire in a charcoal grill with a cover, or preheat a gas grill to medium high.

To prepare the fennel, place the fennel rings in a bowl, add the lemon juice, oil, and salt, and toss. Place the fennel in a grill basket and cook on the grill, shaking the basket occasionally, until soft, 10 to 12 minutes. Transfer the fennel to a sheet of aluminum foil, sprinkle with the lemon zest, and wrap in the foil to keep warm.

In a heavy fireproof skillet, cook the bacon on the grill until crisp. Transfer to paper towels to

continued

drain and then wrap in foil to keep warm. Wipe out the skillet and set aside.

To make the patties, combine all the ingredients in a large bowl. Handling the meat as little as possible to avoid compacting it, mix well. Form the mixture into 6 equal patties to fit the buns.

Brush the grill rack with vegetable oil. Place the patties on the rack, cover, and cook, turning once, until done to preference, about 5 minutes on each side for medium. During the last few minutes of cooking, place the cheese slices on the patties to melt, and place the buns, cut side down, on the outer edges of the rack to toast lightly. Cover the patties and buns with aluminum foil to keep warm while you prepare the topping.

To make the topping, place the walnuts in the skillet and toast on the grill until golden and fragrant. Whisk the vinegar with the oil in a small bowl and season with salt to taste. Combine the figs, arugula, and toasted walnuts in a bowl. Toss with just enough dressing to coat.

To assemble the burgers, on each bun bottom, place grilled fennel, a patty, 2 bacon slices, and the topping. Add the bun tops and serve.

Heirloom Tomato Salad

This salad is all about using dead-ripe tomatoes just picked from the garden or a farm stand. Choose a variety of colors and sizes to create an interesting display. We've added some great Greek ingredients, but you can create your own special version by changing the cheese, herb, and nuts, and perhaps adding a splash of vinegar or an interesting pesto. **Serves 6**

About 10 assorted heirloom tomatoes, such as Brandywine, Green Zebra, and Purple Cherokee
1 cup assorted cherry tomatoes, such as Green Grape, Yellow Pear, and Sweet 100
2 tablespoons minced fresh oregano
$1/2$ cup (about 2 ounces) crumbled feta cheese
$1/2$ cup pitted and chopped kalamata olives
$1/4$ cup toasted pine nuts
$1/4$ cup fruity extra-virgin olive oil
Kosher or coarse sea salt, for sprinkling
Freshly ground black pepper, for sprinkling

Slice the heirloom tomatoes and arrange attractively on a serving platter. Scatter the cherry tomatoes over the sliced ones. Sprinkle with the oregano, cheese, olives, and nuts. Just before serving, drizzle with the oil and sprinkle with salt and pepper to taste.

Grilled Marinated Vegetables *with Balsamic Syrup*

We've listed an assortment of vegetables, but substitute whatever you find in your garden or local farmers' market. Use inexpensive balsamic vinegar to make the syrup, and save the good stuff for other purposes. **Serves 6**

Marinade
3 tablespoons olive oil
2 tablespoons soy sauce
2 tablespoons freshly squeezed lemon juice
1 tablespoon finely minced fresh thyme
4 teaspoons minced garlic

3 zucchini, quartered lengthwise
3 Japanese eggplants, halved lengthwise
2 red bell peppers, quartered, seeds and
   membranes removed
2 yellow bell peppers, quartered, seeds and
   membranes removed
2 sweet onions, such as Vidalia or Walla Walla,
   cut crosswise into $1/2$-inch slices (keep intact)
8 ounces cremini mushrooms, stems trimmed
8 ounces asparagus, tough ends removed
Kosher or coarse sea salt, for sprinkling
Freshly ground black pepper, for sprinkling

Syrup
1 cup balsamic vinegar
1 tablespoon sugar

To make the marinade, combine all the ingredients in a small bowl and whisk to blend.

Arrange all the vegetables on 1 or 2 baking sheets, drizzle with the marinade, turn until the vegetables are completely coated, and sprinkle with salt and pepper to taste. Cover and refrigerate for about 3 hours.

To make the syrup, combine the vinegar and sugar in a nonreactive saucepan. Bring to a simmer over medium heat, then adjust the heat to maintain a simmer and cook until reduced to about $1/4$ cup, about 15 minutes; use a heatproof measuring cup to check the quantity. Remove from the heat and let cool. Transfer the syrup to a squirt bottle, if available, or a liquid measuring cup.

Prepare a medium fire in a charcoal grill with a cover, or preheat a gas grill to medium.

Brush the grill rack with vegetable oil. Arrange the vegetables on the grill rack (you may have to grill them in 2 batches), cover, and cook, turning occasionally, until crisp-tender and nicely marked.

To serve, arrange the warm vegetables on a warm platter (if necessary, return the vegetables to the baking sheet, and place in a hot oven for a minute to warm through) and drizzle with the syrup.

Buttermilk Panna Cotta *with Honeyed Berries*

Local dairy products, honey, and garden-ripe berries are highlighted in this refreshing dessert.
Serves 6

Panna Cotta

1 envelope (1 scant tablespoon) unflavored gelatin

1/4 cup milk (not nonfat)

1 1/2 cups heavy whipping cream

1/2 cup sugar

1 1/2 cups buttermilk

1 teaspoon pure vanilla extract

3 cups mixed seasonal berries, such as blackberries, blueberries, and raspberries

2 tablespoons honey, preferably locally produced

Pesticide-free edible flowers, such as borage, violets, or Johnny-jump-ups, for garnish

To make the panna cotta, combine the gelatin and milk in a small bowl. Stir well and set aside to soften.

Meanwhile, combine the cream and sugar in a saucepan. Heat over medium heat, stirring frequently, until the mixture comes to a boil. Stir in the softened gelatin and cook, stirring, until the mixture is smooth and the gelatin is completely dissolved, about 1 minute. Remove from the heat and let cool to room temperature.

Stir the buttermilk and vanilla into the cream mixture. Pour through a fine-mesh strainer into a pitcher or large liquid measuring cup and discard the solids. Then, pour the mixture evenly into 6 (6-ounce) custard cups or ramekins. Cover tightly with plastic wrap and refrigerate until set, at least 3 hours.

About 30 minutes before serving, gently toss the berries with the honey in a bowl. Taste and add more honey, if desired.

To serve, dip the base of a custard cup into hot water for about 30 seconds, run a small sharp knife around the inside edge of the cup, and invert the panna cotta directly onto an individual plate. Repeat with the remaining cups. Spoon the berries around the panna cotta and garnish with flowers.

Game Plan
Evening of Sports, Cards, or Boards

We offer two options for a game-night party.
Plan one: gather your favorite sports fans to watch a big game on TV. Plan two: organize an evening of board or card games. Our menu works either way.

If you're going the sports route, arrange comfortable seating in front of the TV, choose dishes and napkins in your team's colors, and provide trays for diners.

For the board or card game option, set up small tables for convivial conversation during supper and play, and use two colors of plates and table linens to divide the group into two teams for competitive gaming. If you wish to have music while dining and playing, choose some high-energy pop or rock to keep the evening lively.

Buffalo, or bison, is no longer considered "wild game," but the ranch-raised meat makes a winning burger for our game-night theme. Since everyone enjoys snacking while watching or playing a game, we suggest three tasty dips and a big bowl of "wine nuts" (instead of the usual beer nuts). Whether guests are watching the Super Bowl, playing a winning hand of cards, or rolling the dice for a Boardwalk hotel, our super sundae bowls will score big during halftime or a break in the game playing.

MENU

Chips with a Trio of Dips

Spiced Wine Nuts

Sutter Home Chardonnay
Sutter Home White Zinfandel

Home on the Range Buffalo Burgers *with Fresh Garden Herbs and Huntsman Cheese*

Sutter Home Cabernet Sauvignon
Sutter Home Merlot

Brownie Bowl Sundaes

Chips with a Trio of Dips

Choose sturdy potato or corn chips, or both, for dipping into these three flavorful blends. **Serves 6**

Sun-Dried Tomato Dip

8 ounces cream cheese

1/2 cup mayonnaise

1/2 cup sour cream

1/4 cup drained and finely chopped oil-packed sun-dried tomatoes

1 tablespoon tomato paste, preferably sun-dried

1/4 cup coarsely chopped basil leaves

1/4 teaspoon hot sauce

1/2 teaspoon kosher or coarse sea salt

1/4 teaspoon freshly ground black pepper

Herbed Crème Fraîche Dip

8 ounces crème fraîche

8 ounces cream cheese

2 teaspoons finely grated fresh lemon zest

1 tablespoon freshly squeezed lemon juice

1/2 teaspoon kosher or coarse sea salt

2 tablespoons finely chopped fresh chives

2 tablespoons finely chopped fresh tarragon

2 tablespoons finely chopped fresh flat-leaf parsley

Minced fresh chives, tarragon, and parsley, for sprinkling

Guacamole

2 ripe California Hass avocados

1 tablespoon freshly squeezed lime juice

2 tablespoons chopped pickled jalapeño chiles

1 tablespoon minced garlic

1 tablespoon finely chopped fresh cilantro leaves

1/4 cup finely chopped vine-ripened tomato

1/4 cup finely chopped white onion

1/2 teaspoon kosher or coarse sea salt

Chips, for serving

To make the tomato dip, combine all the ingredients in a food processor and process until well blended. Taste and add more hot sauce, salt, and pepper, if desired. Cover and refrigerate until well chilled.

To make the crème fraîche dip, combine the crème fraîche, cheese, lemon zest, lemon juice, and salt in a food processor and process until well blended. Transfer to a bowl and fold in the chives, tarragon, and parsley. Taste and add more salt, if desired. Cover and refrigerate until well chilled. Sprinkle with the minced herbs just before serving.

To make the guacamole, scoop the avocado flesh into a bowl. Add the lime juice, chiles, garlic, and cilantro and run a table knife repeatedly through the avocado to get a smooth, yet slightly chunky, texture. Stir in the tomato, onion, and salt. Taste and add more lime juice, chiles, and salt, if desired. If not serving immediately, place plastic wrap directly onto the surface of the guacamole, sealing out air as much as possible to prevent oxidation and discoloration, and refrigerate for up to a few hours.

To serve, transfer each dip to a serving bowl and surround the bowls with plenty of chips.

Spiced Wine Nuts

For our riff on the usual beer nuts, any combination of nuts—cashews, hazelnuts (filberts), pecans, peanuts, pistachios, and others—may be used. This roasted mix with a sweet-spicy crunch tastes great with wine. **Serves 6**

2 pounds assorted raw nuts
$1/2$ cup sugar
1 cup water
2 teaspoons kosher or coarse sea salt
$1/2$ teaspoon cayenne pepper

Preheat the oven to 350°F.

Spread the nuts in a single layer on a rimmed baking sheet and roast, stirring occasionally, until lightly browned, 10 to 15 minutes.

Meanwhile, combine $1/4$ cup of the sugar with the water in a large sauté pan. Bring to a simmer over medium heat, stirring to dissolve the sugar, then adjust the heat to maintain a simmer, and cook until reduced to about $1/4$ cup, about 10 minutes; use a heatproof measuring cup to check the quantity, and then return the syrup to the pan.

While the nuts are still hot, transfer them to the syrup in the pan and stir constantly until all the liquid is absorbed. Immediately sprinkle with the remaining $1/4$ cup sugar and the salt, and stir until the nuts are evenly coated. Sprinkle with the cayenne and toss to coat evenly. Transfer the nuts back to the baking sheet, spread them out, and let them cool completely.

To serve, pour the cooled nuts into a serving bowl.

Home on the Range Buffalo Burgers

with Fresh Garden Herbs and Huntsman Cheese

"The original campfire burger had to be made from buffalo meat," says Rick Rohr of Darien, Connecticut, who was an Alternative Burger finalist in Sutter Home Winery's Build a Better Burger contest in 2007. Noting that buffalo is now "gaining in popularity, with its associated health benefits, and more readily available," Rick found it "only natural to develop an alternative burger using buffalo. With buffalo being a bit lean, I added some beef into the mix. Since I used two of the best ground meats, I thought I would team them with two favorite cheeses by using the classic Huntsman cheese. A savory blend of herbs rounds out the burger." **Serves 6**

Mayonnaise
3/4 cup mayonnaise
1/4 cup sour cream
1/2 cup minced fresh flat-leaf parsley
1/3 cup chopped fresh chives
2 teaspoons chopped fresh tarragon
2 teaspoons minced garlic
2 teaspoons chopped anchovy fillets

Patties
1 1/2 pounds ground buffalo (bison)
1/2 pound ground beef chuck
1/4 cup thick-and-creamy-style horseradish
1/2 cup grated red onion
1 1/2 teaspoons salt

12 ounces Huntsman cheese (Stilton layered with double Gloucester), cut into 6 equal slices
6 cracked-wheat hamburger buns, split
6 tablespoons honey mustard
4 cups coarsely chopped European-style salad mix

Prepare a medium-hot fire in a charcoal grill with a cover, or preheat a gas grill to medium high.

To make the mayonnaise, combine all the ingredients in a food processor and pulse about 10 times to blend. Transfer to a small bowl, cover, and refrigerate until assembling the burgers.

To make the patties, combine the buffalo, beef, horseradish, onion, and salt in a large bowl. Handling the meat as little as possible to avoid compacting it, mix well. Form the mixture into 6 equal patties to fit the buns.

Brush the grill rack with vegetable oil. Place the patties on the rack, cover, and cook, turning once, until done to preference, about 5 minutes on each side for medium. During the last few minutes of cooking, place the cheese slices on the patties to melt, and place the buns, cut side down, on the outer edges of the rack to toast lightly.

To assemble the burgers, spread the mustard over the bun bottoms and the mayonnaise over the bun tops. On each bun bottom, place the salad mix and a patty. Add the bun tops and serve.

Brownie Bowl Sundaes

You might choose to add a rich chocolate sauce when assembling the sundaes. Or you could put out several ice creams and a variety of sauces and other toppings and let guests create their own top-scoring versions. **Serves 6**

Brownies

4 ounces unsweetened chocolate, coarsely chopped

1/4 cup (1/2 stick) unsalted butter, cut into small pieces

1 1/2 cups sugar

2 eggs, at room temperature

1 teaspoon pure vanilla extract

1/4 teaspoon salt

1 cup all-purpose flour

Sauce

1 1/2 cups firmly packed light brown sugar

3/4 cup heavy whipping cream

3/4 cup (1 1/2 sticks) unsalted butter

1/4 teaspoon salt

1 quart coffee or vanilla ice cream

1 1/2 cups pecans, cashews, or other nuts, lightly toasted and coarsely chopped

Whipped cream, for serving

To make the brownies, preheat the oven to 350°F. Butter an 8-inch square baking pan.

Combine the chocolate and butter in a large stainless-steel bowl. Bring about 1 inch of water to a bare simmer in a large skillet or shallow saucepan, and set the bowl of chocolate mixture in it. Stir gently until the mixture is melted and smooth. Remove from the heat and let cool for about 10 minutes.

Add the sugar, eggs, vanilla, and salt to the cooled chocolate mixture and mix until well blended. Add the flour and mix gently just until incorporated. Scrape the batter into the baking pan and spread evenly. Bake until a skewer inserted halfway between the edge of the pan and the center comes out only slightly moist with a few crumbs attached, about 25 minutes. Let cool completely in the pan on a wire rack, and then cut into 6 equal portions.

To make the sauce, combine all the ingredients in a small saucepan and cook over medium heat, stirring constantly, until the sugar is dissolved and the butter is melted, 4 to 5 minutes.

To assemble, break each brownie into large chunks and place in a serving bowl or goblet. Add a scoop or two of the ice cream and spoon on some of the sauce, nuts, and whipped cream. Serve immediately.

Jamaican Me Hungry
Caribbean Cookout

A party with a Caribbean beat guarantees a spicy time for all!

Jerk is Jamaica's name for either wet or dry spice mixtures used to flavor meat, poultry, or seafood, and is also the term for the method of grilling or barbecuing the seasoned foods. Some island residents say the name comes from the frequent turning, or jerking, of the meat on the grill, yet others maintain that the name originated from barbecued pork being pulled, or jerked, apart after cooking. No matter the roots, jerk means highly flavorful food, as evidenced by the jerk burgers that anchor this menu.

To create a lively, casual table, use the cool blues and greens of the sea and the tropical island landscape, accented with the vibrant hues of hot pink, red, turquoise, and yellow that Jamaicans use to paint their buildings and food carts. Hibiscus, known as *jamaica* throughout Latin America, is a perfect choice for flowers, as are any other tropical blossoms and leaves. Play calypso and reggae music to add even more color and spice to the revelry.

MENU

Kingston Breezes

Pineapple Upside-Down Jerk Burgers

Cinnamon-Roasted Sweet Potatoes

Hearts of Palm and Peppadew Salad

Sutter Home Gewürztraminer
Sutter Home Sauvignon Blanc
Sutter Home White Merlot

Key Lime Puddings

Sutter Home Moscato

Kingston Breezes

Refreshing as the wind off the Caribbean!
Serves 6

8 limes
2 (750-ml) bottles Sutter Home Sauvignon
  Blanc
$^1/3$ cup sugar
Crushed ice, for serving

Quarter each lime lengthwise, cut each quarter
crosswise into slices about $^1/4$ inch thick, and
transfer to a pitcher. Add the wine and sugar and
stir until the sugar is dissolved. Taste and add
more sugar, if desired. Cover and refrigerate for at
least 4 hours for the limes to infuse the wine.

To serve, pour over crushed ice into 6 high-
ball glasses.

Pineapple Upside-Down Jerk Burgers

Austin, Texas, resident Gina Wilson made this Caribbean-inspired burger at the 2005 Sutter Home Winery's Build a Better Burger Cook-Off. "Celebrating the fresh fruits of the season," Gina explains, "this spicy-sweet combination is the perfect summer burger recipe. The highly seasoned, moist patties have just the right amount of spicy heat, and the sweetness of the pineapple on one side of the meat and mango on the other side complements it well. The buttery mango–avocado salsa adds a nice creamy texture, and the lightly toasted jalapeño bun is perfect for this tropical version of an American tradition." Look for jalapeño buns in the bakery section of many large supermarkets. **Serves 6**

Mayonnaise
6 tablespoons mayonnaise
1 tablespoon freshly squeezed lime juice

Salsa
2 ripe mangoes, finely chopped
1 large or 2 small ripe avocados, finely chopped
3 tablespoons finely chopped fresh cilantro
1 tablespoon finely chopped jalapeño chile
2 tablespoons freshly squeezed lime juice

Jerk Marinade
1 cup chopped fresh cilantro
1 cup chopped fresh flat-leaf parsley
1/2 cup chopped green onions, including green tops
1 tablespoon seeded and chopped Scotch bonnet or habanero chile
2 tablespoons coarsely chopped garlic
2 teaspoons grated fresh ginger
1 tablespoon ground allspice
1 tablespoon dried thyme
1 teaspoon ground cloves
Pinch of ground cinnamon
2 tablespoons olive oil
1/4 cup red wine vinegar
2 tablespoons Sutter Home Zinfandel
1/4 cup soy sauce
2 tablespoons water
2 tablespoons light or dark brown sugar
2 tablespoons freshly squeezed lime juice

Patties
2 pounds ground sirloin
2 teaspoons kosher or coarse sea salt
1/2 cup prepared Jerk Marinade (recipe above)

6 cored fresh pineapple rings, 1/2 inch thick
6 jalapeño buns, split

Prepare a medium-hot fire in a charcoal grill with a cover, or preheat a gas grill to medium high.

To make the mayonnaise, combine the ingredients in a small bowl and mix well. Cover and refrigerate until assembling the burgers.

To make the salsa, combine all the ingredients in a bowl and mix well.

To make the marinade, combine all the ingredients in a food processor and blend until finely minced and mixed through.

To make the patties, combine the beef, salt, and 1/2 cup of marinade in a large bowl. (The rest of the marinade will be used for grilling.) Handling the meat as little as possible to avoid compacting it, mix well. Form the mixture into 6 equal patties to fit the buns.

continued

Pineapple Upside-Down Jerk Burgers, *continued*

Brush the grill rack with vegetable oil. Place the pineapple rings on the rack. Brush with reserved marinade and cook for 2 to 3 minutes. Turn the rings, brush with marinade again, and cook until heated through, another 2 to 3 minutes. Remove from the grill and cover with aluminum foil to keep warm until assembling the burgers.

Place the patties on the rack and brush with marinade. Cover and cook, turning once and brushing with marinade, until done to preference, about 5 minutes per side for medium. During the last few minutes of cooking, place the rolls, cut side down, on the outer edges of the rack to toast lightly.

To assemble the burgers, lightly spread the mayonnaise over the cut sides of the buns. On each bun bottom, place a pineapple ring, a patty, and salsa. Add the bun tops and serve.

Cinnamon-Roasted Sweet Potatoes

We prefer regular sweet potatoes with pale yellow flesh for this preparation, but orange-fleshed yam varieties may be used. **Serves 6**

1 tablespoon ground cinnamon
1 tablespoon kosher or coarse sea salt
2 teaspoons sugar
$1/2$ teaspoon finely ground black pepper
$1/4$ teaspoon ground cayenne
$2 1/2$ pounds sweet potatoes
3 tablespoons olive oil
1 tablespoon chopped fresh flat-leaf parsley

Preheat the oven to 450°F. Grease 1 or 2 rimmed baking sheets with cooking spray.

Combine the cinnamon, salt, sugar, black pepper, and cayenne in a small bowl and mix thoroughly.

Peel the sweet potatoes, trim the pointed ends, and cut crosswise into $1/2$-inch-thick rounds. Combine the potatoes and oil in a large bowl and toss to coat well. Sprinkle in the cinnamon mixture and toss until evenly distributed. Place the rounds in a single layer on the baking sheets. Roast until lightly browned on the bottoms, 10 to 15 minutes; check early to prevent overbrowning. Turn with a spatula (you may need to gently pry the rounds loose) and continue roasting until tender, about 5 minutes longer; be careful not to let the cinnamon burn. Remove the baking sheets to a wire rack to cool slightly.

To serve, transfer the potatoes to a serving platter and sprinkle with the parsley.

Hearts of Palm and Peppadew Salad

Fresh hearts of palm are readily available in Florida and Hawaii and in some specialty markets elsewhere. *Peppadew* is the trademarked name given to the processed South African fruit that resembles a cross between a sweet pepper and a tomato. Bottled Peppadews (or loose ones in "olive bars") and canned hearts of palm are sold in many upscale markets. **Serves 6**

1/2 pound fresh hearts of palm, peeled, or 1 (14.5-ounce) can hearts of palm, drained

1 lemon, halved crosswise (if using fresh palm hearts)

1 bay leaf (if using fresh palm hearts)

1 teaspoon black peppercorns (if using fresh palm hearts)

1 teaspoon kosher or coarse sea salt (if using fresh palm hearts)

2 cups water (if using fresh palm hearts)

8 ounces chayote squash, peeled, seeded, and cut into julienne

4 ounces Peppadews, drained and cut into eighths

1/4 cup pitted niçoise olives

1/4 cup slivered red onion

1 tablespoon chopped fresh flat-leaf parsley

1 tablespoon chiffonade-cut fresh basil leaves

Finely grated zest of 2 oranges

Vinaigrette

1/4 cup extra-virgin olive oil

2 tablespoons sherry vinegar

1/2 teaspoon kosher or coarse sea salt

1/4 teaspoon freshly ground black pepper

Pinch of crushed red chile flakes

Pinch of sugar

Prepare a medium-hot fire in a charcoal grill with a cover, or preheat a gas grill to medium high.

If using fresh hearts of palm, combine the lemon, bay leaf, peppercorns, salt, and water in a saucepan and bring to a boil over medium-high heat. Add the palm hearts and cook for 2 minutes to blanch. Drain and transfer to a bowl of iced water to halt the cooking; then drain again.

Slice the blanched or canned palm hearts in half lengthwise. Brush the grill rack with vegetable oil. Place the palm hearts on the rack, cover, and cook, turning once, until nicely marked on both sides, about 2 minutes on each side. Slice lengthwise into strips about 1/8 inch thick.

Combine the palm hearts, chayote, Peppadews, olives, onion, parsley, basil, and orange zest in a bowl. Cover and refrigerate until chilled.

To make the vinaigrette, combine all the ingredients in a small bowl, and whisk to blend well. Taste and add more salt and pepper, if desired.

To serve, toss the salad with the vinaigrette and transfer to a serving bowl.

Key Lime Puddings

The lime that is native to India and Malaysia and is now known as *key* or *Mexican lime* made its way to the Caribbean via Spanish settlers. Long cultivated in Florida, these uniquely fragrant little fruits are now shipped all over and can be found in many supermarkets or Latin markets. Look for those that are turning yellow, as the green ones are very tart. If key limes are unavailable, commonly available Persian limes (sold simply as "limes" in supermarkets) are a much better substitute than bottled key lime juice.

If you're worried about the presence of salmonella in raw eggs in your area, use pasteurized eggs. **Serves 6**

4 egg yolks

1 (14-ounce) can sweetened condensed milk (not evaporated milk)

1/2 cup freshly squeezed lime juice, preferably key or Mexican lime varieties

2 tablespoon finely grated fresh lime zest

1 cup heavy whipping cream

2 tablespoons confectioners' sugar

1/2 teaspoon pure vanilla extract

2 cups crushed crisp sugar or coconut cookies (6.75-ounce package)

6 thin lime slices, for garnish

Place the egg yolks in a bowl and whisk until pale yellow. Add the milk, juice, and zest and whisk until smooth. Cover and refrigerate until set, about 4 hours or overnight.

Pour the cream into a bowl and beat with a whisk or an electric mixer just until the cream begins to thicken. Add the sugar and vanilla and continue to beat just until the cream holds its shape well; be very careful not to overbeat if using an electric mixer.

Layer the cookie crumbs, lime pudding, and cream into 6 (6-ounce) glasses, dividing evenly. Refrigerate until ready to serve, at least 1 hour.

Garnish with the lime slices and serve chilled.

Moroccan Mystique
Supper in the Moonlight

Check the calendar for an upcoming full moon night, and choose the most romantic spot you can for this party. A courtyard or patio with a fountain is an ideal setting, but no matter where you stage the evening, fill the space with twinkling candles and lots of roses.

When inviting guests, suggest that they wear djellabas or caftans, if they have access to these typical Moroccan robes, or glittery belly-dance outfits if they dare. For those who wish to go all out, authentic North African garb can be rented from costume suppliers.

You may wish to create a tent effect around the dining area by hanging lengths of gauzy fabric overhead and draping it across to walls or a fence where it can be attached. For dining, use a large coffee table, drape it with a cloth to the ground, overlay that with a shimmering sheer fabric in a metallic hue, and pile large pillows around for relaxed seating.

Moroccan music is essential to transport everyone to North Africa for the evening. To add a festive note, check your local listings for a belly dancer, or check with a dance school that offers classes in this art.

Shortly before guests arrive, slip into your costume, and sprinkle fresh rose petals over the tabletop and everywhere.

Go as far as you wish in creating Moroccan mystique, but the more you do to conjure up an exotic atmosphere, the more fun everyone will have.

MENU

Hot Dates

Moroccan Marinated Olives

Sutter Home Chenin Blanc
Sutter Home Sauvignon Blanc

Sweet and Spicy Red Fez Burgers *with Marrakesh Carrot Salad and Chermoula Mayonnaise*

Saffron Couscous *with Watercress and Dried Apricots*

Orange and Sugar Snap Pea Salad

Sutter Home Chardonnay
Sutter Home Merlot
Sutter Home Red

Pistachio-Anise Shortcakes *with Meyer Lemon Curd and Figs*

Sutter Home Moscato

Hot Dates

Prepare and serve this simple appetizer when you fire up the grill for the burgers, and enjoy the contrasting salty cheese and sweet dates. **Serves 6**

18 large pitted dried dates, preferably Medjool variety

About 5 ounces mild feta cheese, cut into 18 pieces

Olive oil, for brushing

Honey, for drizzling

Ground cayenne, for dusting

Prepare a medium fire in a charcoal grill with a cover, or preheat a gas grill to medium.

Stuff each date with a piece of the cheese. Brush the dates lightly with oil and place on the grill rack. Cover and cook until heated through, 1 to 2 minutes. Remove to a serving plate, drizzle with honey, and dust lightly with cayenne to taste. Serve immediately.

Moroccan Marinated Olives

Be sure to use tree-ripened olives—which may be various shades of green, purple, or black—that have been cured in brine. Choose one kind or a mixture, but avoid the mild-flavored canned California ripe olives. **Serves 6**

2 cups brine-cured olives such as niçoise

3 tablespoons extra-virgin olive oil

3 tablespoons freshly squeezed lemon juice

1 teaspoon minced garlic

2 tablespoons chopped fresh cilantro

1 tablespoon chopped fresh flat-leaf parsley

1 teaspoon ground cumin

1 teaspoon kosher or coarse sea salt

1/2 teaspoon freshly ground black pepper

1/4 teaspoon ground cayenne

Rinse the olives in a strainer under cold running water and drain well. On a cutting board, pound the olives lightly with a meat tenderizer or other blunt instrument to crack the skins so that the seasonings will penetrate.

Transfer the olives to a stainless-steel or other nonreactive bowl. Add the remaining ingredients and mix well. Taste and add more salt, pepper, and cayenne, if desired. Cover with plastic wrap and let stand at room temperature for at least 12 hours, stirring occasionally.

Transfer to a serving bowl and serve.

Sweet and Spicy Red Fez Burgers

with Marrakesh Carrot Salad and Chermoula Mayonnaise

"This burger celebrates the collaboration of our American burger with the bold and vibrant flavors of Morocco," wrote Barry Rosenstein, the Sutter Home Winery's 2005 Build a Better Burger Grand Prize winner from Elmhurst, Illinois. "It perfectly balances sweet and spicy and always leaves my guests asking for the recipe. The signature touch of red food color to paint the roll tops is a tribute to my grandfather, who would always take us kids to see the Shriners' circus, where it seemed like everyone was wearing a red fez."

Harissa, a North African hot sauce, is available in many major supermarkets and Mediterranean groceries. *Chermoula* is a thick blend of herbs and spices used in North Africa as a condiment or marinade; Barry's recipe blends chermoula ingredients with mayonnaise for a quick and easy condiment. *Merguez*, a North African sausage made from lamb, may be found in charcuteries or upscale meat markets, or you can make your own (see page 116). **Serves 6**

6 Kaiser rolls, split
Red food coloring, for brushing

Mayonnaise
1/2 cup chopped fresh cilantro
4 cloves garlic, crushed
1 teaspoon ground cumin
1 teaspoon ground paprika
1 teaspoon harissa
2 tablespoons freshly squeezed lemon juice
1 teaspoon kosher or coarse sea salt
6 tablespoons olive oil
1 cup mayonnaise

Carrot Salad
Juice of 1 lemon
2 teaspoons minced garlic
1 teaspoon ground cumin
1/4 teaspoon ground cinnamon
1/2 teaspoon ground paprika
1/4 teaspoon crushed red chile flakes
1 teaspoon kosher or coarse sea salt
1 teaspoon honey
1 teaspoon chopped fresh flat-leaf parsley
2 tablespoons olive oil
1 pound carrots, peeled and grated

Patties
1 1/2 pounds ground chuck
1/2 pound merguez (North African–style lamb sausage), casing discarded
2 ounces dried apricots, diced
2 ounces pitted dried dates, diced
1 1/2 teaspoons ground cumin
1 teaspoon ground cinnamon
3 tablespoons chopped fresh cilantro
3 tablespoons chopped fresh mint
2 teaspoons harissa
2 teaspoons kosher or coarse sea salt
1/2 teaspoon freshly ground black pepper

3 cups shredded romaine lettuce

Prepare a medium-hot fire in a charcoal grill with a cover, or preheat a gas grill to medium high.

Pour about a tablespoon of the food coloring into a small bowl. Place the roll tops on several layers of paper toweling and brush the

continued

tops with food coloring to cover completely. Set aside to dry.

To make the mayonnaise, combine the cilantro, garlic, cumin, paprika, *harissa*, lemon juice, salt, and oil in a food processor and process until well blended. Transfer to a small bowl and fold in the mayonnaise. Cover and refrigerate until assembling the burgers.

To make the salad, combine the lemon juice, garlic, cumin, cinnamon, paprika, chile flakes, and salt in a bowl. Mix well to combine. Add the honey, parsley, olive oil, and carrots and mix well. Cover and refrigerate until assembling the burgers.

To make the patties, combine all the ingredients in a large bowl. Handling the meat as little as possible to avoid compacting it, mix well. Form the mixture into 6 equal patties to fit the rolls.

Brush the grill rack with vegetable oil. Place the patties on the rack, cover, and cook, turning once, until done to preference, about 5 minutes on each side for medium. During the last few minutes of cooking, place the rolls, cut side down, on the outer edges of the rack to toast lightly.

To assemble the burgers, drain the carrot salad and squeeze out excess moisture with your hands. Spread a generous amount of the mayonnaise over the cut sides of the rolls. On each roll bottom, place shredded romaine, a patty, and some carrot salad. Add the roll tops and serve.

If you can't locate *merguez* sausage, substitute 1/2 pound ground lamb, increase the cilantro to 1/4 cup, and add 1 teaspoon minced garlic, 1/4 teaspoon ground fennel, 1/4 teaspoon ground coriander, and 1/4 teaspoon cayenne to the patty mixture.

Orange and Sugar Snap Pea Salad

Be sure to use very tender peas in this refreshing salad. **Serves 6**

6 navel oranges
2 cups young, tender sugar snap peas, trimmed
1 cup slivered almonds, toasted
1/2 cup chiffonade-cut fresh mint leaves
1/2 cup extra-virgin olive oil
4 teaspoons orange blossom water
4 teaspoons white balsamic vinegar
Kosher or coarse sea salt

Peel the oranges with a sharp knife, removing all the white pith. Working over a stainless-steel or other nonreactive bowl to collect the juices, cut between the membranes to remove each segment and place the segments in another nonreactive bowl.

To the bowl of segments, add 1/2 cup of the collected juice and the remaining ingredients, including salt to taste, and toss to coat well. Cover and refrigerate for 1 hour before serving. Just before serving, toss again and transfer to a serving bowl.

Saffron Couscous *with Watercress and Dried Apricots*

Enjoy this colorful side dish at room temperature. To make certain that the couscous doesn't turn into mush while absorbing the hot liquid, buy readily available quick-cooking couscous, which is steamed and then dried before packaging.

Serves 6

3/4 cup freshly squeezed orange juice

1 teaspoon ground ginger

1 teaspoon ground cinnamon

1/8 teaspoon saffron

3/4 cup water

1 1/2 cups packaged quick-cooking (instant) couscous, preferably Near East brand

1 1/2 cups watercress, larger stems removed

12 dried apricots, thinly sliced

1/2 cup toasted pine nuts

1/4 cup thinly sliced green onions, including green tops

6 tablespoons fruity extra-virgin olive oil

1 teaspoon finely grated fresh lemon zest

2 tablespoons freshly squeezed lemon juice

1 teaspoons kosher or coarse sea salt

1/4 teaspoon freshly ground black pepper

Combine the orange juice, ginger, cinnamon, saffron, and water in a saucepan. Bring just to a boil over medium heat. Put the couscous in a large bowl, pour in the hot liquid, and stir well. Cover tightly and let stand for 10 minutes.

Uncover the couscous and fluff it gently with a fork. Add the watercress, apricots, nuts, and green onions and toss. Add the oil, lemon zest, lemon juice, salt, and pepper and mix well. Taste and add more salt and pepper, if desired.

To serve, mound the couscous on a serving plate or transfer to a serving bowl.

Pistachio-Anise Shortcakes *with Meyer Lemon Curd and Figs*

Anise, pistachios, and thin-skinned lemons, such as Meyer variety, are all prized by Moroccan cooks, and Jeffrey captured these flavors in these short-cakes. When figs are out of season, substitute fresh berries, apricots, nectarines, or peaches.

Serves 6

Lemon Curd

6 egg yolks

1 cup sugar

2/3 cup freshly squeezed lemon juice, preferably Meyer variety

1 tablespoon finely grated fresh lemon zest, preferably Meyer variety

1/2 cup (1 stick) unsalted butter, cut into several pieces

Shortcakes

1 1/2 cups all-purpose flour

1/4 cup granulated sugar

1 tablespoon baking powder

1/2 teaspoon salt

1 cup plus 2 tablespoons heavy whipping cream

1 tablespoon finely minced fresh orange zest

1/2 teaspoon anise extract

1/4 cup finely ground roasted unsalted pistachios

1/4 cup firmly packed light brown sugar

2 cups sliced fresh figs

2 tablespoons sugar

1/2 cup heavy whipping cream

6 fresh mint sprigs for garnish

To make the lemon curd, combine the egg yolks and sugar in a stainless-steel bowl and beat until light and well blended. Stir in the lemon juice. Bring a saucepan of water to a bare simmer, place the bowl over the pan, and cook, stirring and scraping the sides, until the mixture has thickened enough to coat the back of a spoon (your finger should leave a trail when you run it across the spoon) but is still pourable, about 10 minutes. To prevent the eggs from curdling, do not allow the mixture to approach a boil. Pour through a fine-mesh strainer into a bowl and discard the solids. Stir in the lemon zest and butter until the butter is melted and incorporated. Immediately place a piece of plastic wrap directly onto the surface of the curd to prevent a skin from forming. Cool to room temperature, and then cover and refrigerate until chilled.

To make the shortcakes, preheat the oven to 375°F. Line a baking sheet with parchment paper or a silicone baking mat.

Combine the flour, granulated sugar, baking powder, and salt in a bowl and whisk to mix well.

Combine 1 cup of the cream, the orange zest, and the anise in the bowl of an electric mixer. With the whisk attachment, whip on medium-high speed just until soft peaks form. Change to the paddle attachment, add the flour mixture to the cream mixture, and mix on low speed just until all the flour is incorporated, about 10 seconds. Transfer the dough to a lightly floured work surface and knead quickly and gently just until it comes together. Using a ruler as a guide, roll out the dough into a circle about 8 inches in diameter and 1/2 inch thick.

Combine the pistachios and brown sugar in a small bowl. Brush the top of the dough with the remaining 2 tablespoons of the cream and sprinkle on the pistachio mixture. Cut the dough into 6 pie-shaped wedges and place them a few inches apart on the baking sheet. Bake until golden brown, 12 to 15 minutes. Slide the paper or mat off the baking sheet to a wire rack to cool completely.

Shortly before serving, toss the figs with the sugar and let macerate for 5 minutes. Pour the

½ cup cream into a bowl and beat with a whisk or an electric mixer just until the cream is fairly stiff; be very careful not to overbeat if using an electric mixer. Fold the whipped cream into the lemon curd.

To serve, carefully split each of the crumbly shortcakes in half with a serrated knife and place the bottom halves on the centers of 6 dessert plates. Top with the lemon curd and figs and crown with the shortcake tops. Garnish with the mint.

We've merged two popular restaurant experiences—the wine bar and mini burgers—to create a fun celebration that can easily be multiplied to host a large group. When inviting guests, suggest that they dress for a chic night on the town.

Miniature burgers, commonly called *sliders*, are offered at restaurants everywhere these days. Our menu offers three kinds of sliders—beef, chicken, and fish—so that everyone can taste and compare different wines with a variety of little burgers. Setting out an assortment of cheeses plays on the same idea of finding out what works and what doesn't with the various wines. To end the meal, guests can try little bites of dark chocolate with red wines or dip crisp biscotti into a dessert wine.

For a stylish look, pair white and clear glass dishes with elegant bouquets of calla lilies or other white flowers. Put out stacks of small plates and white cocktail napkins for sampling the sliders. Open and display a variety of wines for self-service alongside plenty of clear stemmed glasses for tasting.

To complement the sophisticated atmosphere and menu, play tunes from the Great American Songbook by composers like Cole Porter, George Gershwin, and Irving Berlin, performed by popular past and contemporary artists, like Michael Bublé, Nat "King" Cole, Michael Feinstein, Ella Fitzgerald, Diana Krall, and Frank Sinatra. This might also be the occasion to hire a pianist-vocalist to perform the repertoire.

MENU

Assorted Cheeses

Bouillabaisse Sliders
with Tomato-Fennel Relish and Saffron Mayonnaise

Cobb Sliders

Stuffed Prosciutto Sliders

Assortment of Favorite Wines

Hazelnut Biscotti

Dark Chocolate Truffles

Sutter Home Moscato

ASSORTED CHEESES

When assembling cheeses for a wine tasting, keep in mind that, like all relationships, a successful pairing depends on a healthy balance. It's a common misconception that cheese and wine are a perfect pair, a marriage made in heaven. Not necessarily. A good union can be harmonious and satisfying, but some partnerships can leave a bitter taste in the mouth.

The healthy balance we are looking for when pairing cheese with wine is one of *taste*. When serving a cheese plate with wine, you do not get to use your culinary talents by adding salt, lemon, or anything else to the cheese to bring it into balance with the wine. What you do have to do is pick the correct cheese.

Sweet and umami tastes in food make wines taste *stronger*. These tastes bring out the bitter tannins, acid, and alcohol in wine. They mute the wine's fruit and decrease the sweetness. On the other hand, acid and salty tastes in food make wines taste *milder*. They soften the acid and tannins and make the wine fruitier and sweeter.

Cheese can be divided into two general categories—young/fresh and dry/aged. Most young cheeses have a high concentration of lactose (milk sugar) and glutamates (umami). They are sweet and high in umami, and those tastes

make wine taste stronger. So don't pair these cheeses with strong wines, or else the wines will taste thin and bitter, with muted fruit. For most fresh cheeses, choose mild wines that will not be so adversely affected; varieties like lightly oaked Chardonnay, Chenin Blanc, Gewürztraminer, Riesling, Sauvignon Blanc, White Zinfandel, and sparkling wines work best.

When a cheese is aged, the concentration of salt and acid increases. No longer do sweetness and umami dominate in the cheese. Saltiness and acidity make wines taste milder, so most aged cheeses pair nicely with stronger red wines like Cabernet Sauvignon and Merlot. These cheeses bring out the fruit, soften the tannins, and give the wine a full mouth feel.

Aged cheeses also pair well with most of the milder wines that we recommend with young/fresh cheese. Contrary to traditional belief, white wines are more cheese-friendly than reds. In fact, Riesling, with gobs of fruit perfectly balanced by crisp acidity, low alcohol, and no bitter tannins, may be the most cheese-friendly wine around. And deliciously salty and acidic Parmesan cheese, especially Parmigiano-Reggiano, may be the most wine-friendly cheese. You can pair it with almost any wine.

Use our chart of pairing suggestions on page 126 as a starting point, and don't hesitate to ask for recommendations and samples when buying cheese from a reliable source.

WINES	CHEESES
MILD Chenin Blanc, Gewürztraminer, Moscato, Pinot Grigio, Riesling, Sauvignon Blanc, White Zinfandel	Fresh, young, or slightly aged cheeses: chèvre and other goat cheeses, feta and other sheep cheeses, crescenza, mozzarella di bufala, Mahón, Petit Suisse, Teleme, semisoft blue cheese (with sweet wines)
MEDIUM Chardonnay, Sutter Home Red, White Merlot, Zinfandel	Soft-ripened cheeses (Boursin, Brie, Camembert), double- and triple-cream cheeses (Brillat-Savarin, Explorateur, Saint-André), mild semisoft cheeses (Bel Paese, Comté, Havarti), mild smooth cheeses (Cheddar, Edam, Colby, Gouda, Jarlsberg, Monterey Jack, provolone), washed-rind cheeses (fontina, Pont-l'Évêque, Taleggio), semisoft blue cheeses (with sweet wines and Zinfandel)
STRONG Cabernet Sauvignon, Merlot	Aged cheeses: Asiago, Gouda, Gruyère, Cheddar (medium sharp), Manchego, dry Monterey Jack, Parmesan, semihard blue cheeses

Bouillabaisse Sliders *with Tomato-Fennel Relish and Saffron Mayonnaise*

This recipe from 2006 Sutter Home Winery's Build a Better Burger Alternative Burgers finalist Richard Boulanger of Williston, Vermont, focuses on several key ingredients that would be included in a traditional bouillabaisse. **Serves 6**

Patties
1/2 pound skinless, boneless red snapper fillets (or any other firm-textured lean white fish)
3 ounces peeled and deveined large raw shrimp, cut into about 1/4-inch pieces
2 egg whites
1/2 teaspoon chopped fresh thyme
1/2 teaspoon kosher or coarse sea salt
1/4 teaspoon freshly ground black pepper
1/4 to 1/2 cup panko (Japanese bread crumbs)

Mayonnaise
1/8 teaspoon saffron threads
1 1/2 teaspoons freshly squeezed lemon juice
6 tablespoons mayonnaise
Kosher or coarse sea salt
Freshly ground black pepper

Relish
1/3 cup seeded and finely chopped firm, ripe plum tomato or vine-ripened tomato
5 tablespoons finely chopped fennel bulb
1 1/2 tablespoons finely chopped sweet onion
1/4 teaspoon grated fresh lemon zest
1 1/2 teaspoons freshly squeezed lemon juice
1/2 teaspoon fresh thyme leaves
1 1/2 teaspoons garlic-flavored olive oil
1/8 teaspoon kosher or coarse sea salt
1/8 teaspoon freshly ground black pepper

12 (1/2-inch-thick) slices French bread, cut diagonally from baguettes about 3 inches wide
Garlic-flavored olive oil, for brushing

Prepare a medium-hot fire in a charcoal grill with a cover, or preheat a gas grill to medium high.

Grind the snapper coarsely, in small batches, in a food processor, or chop it by hand into about 1/4-inch pieces. Combine it with the shrimp, egg whites, thyme, salt, and pepper in a bowl and mix well. Stir in enough panko to bind the ingredients together. Form the mixture into 6 equal patties to fit the slices of bread. Cover and refrigerate for at least 30 minutes before cooking.

To make the mayonnaise, combine the saffron and lemon juice in a small bowl and let soak for 20 minutes. Add the mayonnaise and blend until smooth. Season with salt and pepper to taste. Cover and refrigerate.

To make the relish, combine all the ingredients in a small bowl. Cover and refrigerate.

Brush the grill rack with vegetable oil. Place the patties on the rack, cover, and cook, turning once, just until opaque throughout, about 3 minutes on each side. Lightly brush both sides of each slice of bread with garlic-flavored oil and place on the outer edges of the grill rack to toast lightly, turning once.

To assemble the burgers, spread the mayonnaise over one side of each toasted bread slice. Place a patty on 6 of the slices. Using a slotted spoon, top each patty with some tomato-fennel relish. Add the remaining bread slices and serve.

Cobb Sliders

Jay Kakuk of Plymouth, Minnesota, cooked his take on the famed Hollywood Brown Derby's Cobb Salad as a finalist in the 2003 Sutter Home Winery's Build a Better Burger Cook-Off.
Serves 6

Patties
1 pound ground chicken
1/2 cup (about 2 ounces) crumbled blue cheese
4 slices cooked bacon, chopped
1/2 teaspoon chicken seasoning blend

6 dinner rolls, split

Salad
1 1/2 teaspoons olive oil
1 teaspoon freshly squeezed lemon juice
1 teaspoon white wine vinegar
1/2 teaspoon Worcestershire sauce
1/2 teaspoon Dijon mustard
1/2 teaspoon minced garlic
1/4 teaspoon lemon–pepper seasoning
Kosher or coarse sea salt
1/2 cup finely shredded crisp head lettuce, preferably iceberg
1/2 cup diced ripe but firm California Hass avocado
1/2 cup diced tomato
2 slices cooked bacon, crumbled
1 1/2 teaspoons minced fresh chives or green onion tops

Prepare a medium-hot fire in a charcoal grill with a cover, or preheat a gas grill to medium high.

To make the patties, combine all the ingredients in a bowl. Handling the meat as little as possible to avoid compacting it, mix well. Form the mixture into 6 equal patties to fit the rolls.

Brush the grill rack with vegetable oil. Place the patties on the rack, cover, and cook, turning once, just until the juices run clear when the patties are pierced in the center, about 4 minutes on each side. During the last few minutes of cooking, place the rolls, cut side down, on the outer edges of the rack to toast lightly. Cover the patties and rolls with aluminum foil to keep warm while preparing the salad.

To make the salad, combine the oil, lemon juice, vinegar, Worcestershire sauce, mustard, garlic, lemon–pepper seasoning, and salt to taste in a large bowl and whisk until well combined. Add the lettuce, avocado, tomato, bacon, and chives and toss gently.

To assemble the burgers, on each roll bottom, place a patty and top with some salad. Add the roll tops and serve.

Stuffed Prosciutto Sliders

Jenny Flake from Gilbert, Arizona, was a finalist in the 2004 and 2006 Sutter Home Winery's Build a Better Burger Cook-Offs. Enthusiastically describing her 2004 entry, Jenny wrote, "The taste of Italy comes alive with every bite of these ultra-juicy burgers that melt in your mouth. The feta cheese and sun-dried tomatoes stuffed into the patties make the burgers amazingly juicy. The fragrant sweet flavor of the prosciutto adds another great layer of flavor, and the basil mayonnaise brings all of the flavors together beautifully. No one ever guesses how simple these burgers are to prepare! You're hooked after one mouth-watering bite! Enjoy every minute!" **Serves 6**

Mayonnaise
6 tablespoons mayonnaise
1 tablespoon finely chopped fresh basil

Patties
3/4 cup (about 3 ounces) crumbled feta cheese
1/4 cup drained and chopped oil-packed sun-dried tomatoes
1 pound ground sirloin
1 egg, lightly beaten
1 1/2 teaspoons Tabasco pepper sauce
1 tablespoon dried Italian seasoning, crushed
1/2 teaspoon kosher or coarse sea salt
1/4 teaspoon freshly ground pepper
1 1/2 teaspoons minced garlic
1/4 cup Italian-style bread crumbs
1/4 cup (about 1 ounce) freshly grated Parmesan cheese

6 (2 1/2-inch) squares focaccia bread, halved horizontally
6 thin prosciutto slices, folded to fit bread

6 inner leaves romaine lettuce, trimmed to fit bread
6 paper-thin slices red onion, separated into rings

Prepare a medium-hot fire in a charcoal grill with a cover, or preheat a gas grill to medium high.

To make the mayonnaise, combine the ingredients in a small bowl and mix together. Cover and refrigerate until assembling the burgers.

To make the patties, combine the feta and tomatoes in a small bowl. Divide into 6 equal portions, form into balls, and set aside. Combine the ground sirloin, egg, pepper sauce, Italian seasoning, salt, pepper, garlic, bread crumbs, and Parmesan in a bowl. Handling the meat as little as possible to avoid compacting it, mix well. Form the mixture into 12 equal thin patties to fit the bread squares. Place a ball of the feta mixture in the center of 6 of the patties and press down lightly to spread. Place the remaining patties on top, press down lightly, and seal the edges to totally enclose the filling, forming 6 patties total.

Brush the grill rack with vegetable oil. Place the patties on the rack, cover, and cook, turning once, until done to preference, about 5 minutes on each side for medium. During the last few minutes of cooking, place the focaccia squares, cut side down, on the outer edges of the rack to toast lightly.

To assemble the burgers, spread the basil mayonnaise over the cut sides of the bread bottoms. On each bread bottom, place a patty, a prosciutto slice, a lettuce leaf, and some red onion rings. Add the bread tops and serve.

Hazelnut Biscotti

Dry, crunchy, and subtly nutty, these long, elegant Italian cookies are perfect for dipping into sweet dessert wines before nibbling. **Serves 6**

  2 cups all-purpose flour
  1 cup sugar
  2 teaspoons baking powder
  1/4 teaspoon salt
  3 eggs, lightly beaten
  2 teaspoons pure vanilla extract
  1 cup hazelnuts, lightly toasted and coarsely
    chopped

Preheat the oven to 300°F. Line a baking sheet with parchment paper or a silicone baking mat.

In a bowl, combine the flour, sugar, baking powder, and salt and whisk to mix well. Add the eggs and vanilla and mix well with a spoon (the mixture will be crumbly). Stir in the nuts. Transfer the mixture to a lightly floured work surface. Dust your hands with flour and gently knead the dough until it comes together, about 1 minute (the dough will be sticky). Transfer the dough to the baking sheet. Using a ruler as a guide and dusting your hands with flour as needed, shape the dough into an even, flat rectangle about 6 by 9 inches.

Bake until the dough is lightly golden and feels firm when lightly touched in the center, about 50 minutes. (The dough will spread into a large, rounded rectangle as it bakes.) Remove the baking sheet to a wire rack to cool for about 15 minutes, then peel the dough from the paper or mat and transfer it to a cutting board. Wipe any crumbs from the paper or mat and return it to the baking sheet. Using a serrated knife, first slice off and discard the rounded edges of the 2 shorter sides of the dough rectangle to make straight sides, and then slice the rectangle along a shorter side into 3/4-inch-thick slices. Lay each slice with one cut side down on the baking sheet, keeping the slices about 1 inch apart.

Return the baking sheet to the oven and bake until the upper sides of the slices are golden, about 20 minutes. Remove the baking sheet from the oven, turn the biscotti over, return to the oven, and continue baking until the upper sides of the biscotti are golden, about 20 minutes longer. Slide the paper or mat off the baking sheet to a wire rack to cool completely.

To serve, stand the biscotti upright in a bowl or arrange on a plate.

Dark Chocolate Truffles

The original French chocolate truffles, formed from misshapen balls of ganache rolled in cocoa powder, resemble their namesake prized fungus freshly dug from the earth. Be sure to choose excellent chocolate that tastes great on its own.

Serves 6

8 ounces premium dark chocolate (about 70% cacao), finely chopped

1 tablespoon unsalted butter, at room temperature

1/2 cup heavy whipping cream

1 tablespoon light corn syrup

1 tablespoon pure vanilla extract

3 tablespoons cocoa powder

2 tablespoons confectioners' sugar

Place the chocolate and butter in a bowl. Set aside.

Combine the cream and corn syrup in a saucepan and bring just to a boil over medium heat. Pour the mixture over the chocolate and butter and stir until they are melted and the mixture is smooth. Stir in the vanilla, cover, and refrigerate until firm but still soft enough to scoop, 1 to 2 hours.

Line with parchment paper a baking sheet that will fit in the refrigerator. Combine the cocoa powder and confectioners' sugar in a sifter or strainer and sift into a shallow bowl.

Scoop up about 2 teaspoons of the chocolate mixture and roll very quickly between your hands to form an uneven ball. Drop the truffle into the cocoa mixture, shake and rotate the bowl to completely cover the truffle, and transfer the ball to the baking sheet. Form the rest of the truffles the same way.

Refrigerate the sheet of truffles until firm, about 30 minutes, and then transfer the truffles to an airtight container, placing a sheet of waxed paper between each layer. Refrigerate for at least 24 hours and up to 2 weeks.

To serve, transfer the truffles to a serving platter and let return to room temperature before serving.

Southeast Asian Odyssey
Exotic Street Fare Adventure

First-time travelers to Southeast Asia are often amazed by the vast array of little food stalls along the streets where vendors prepare their specialties, which buyers usually consume on the spot. A party featuring a sampling of street foods can be fun anywhere.

To refresh your knowledge of history, the former French colonies of Cambodia, Laos, and Vietnam were known as French Indochina. Burgers Indochine, featured on our menu, pay homage to that region but are definitely not something you'd find for sale on Southeast Asia's city streets. Rather, they were inspired by the baguette sandwiches of flavorful meats and vegetables that are popular in Vietnam. The side dishes and dessert bring in flavors of other Southeast Asian nations.

This is a good menu to serve buffet-style in the kitchen. Scatter some tropical leaves and orchids on the kitchen island or a counter and gather bamboo wooden platters for serving. Reusable bamboo dishes and flatware plus brightly hued napkins add to the tropical theme. You may wish to put out small plates for the burgers and small bamboo bowls for serving the soupy noodles and juicy salad, allowing guests to try one dish at a time as though they were sampling various street vendors' offerings.

An array of Southeast Asian music will impart an authentic background for your culinary adventure.

MENU

Burgers Indochine

Red Curry Rice Noodles

Cucumber-Mushroom Salad
with Tangerine Vinaigrette

Sutter Home Gewürztraminer
Sutter Home Pinot Grigio
Sutter Home Sauvignon Blanc
Sutter Home White Zinfandel

Coconut Tapioca *with Tropical Fruits*

Sutter Home Moscato

Burgers Indochine

These burgers are a riff on the scrumptious Vietnamese *báhn mi* sandwiches of meat and vegetables tucked into crusty French baguettes. They were created by Ellie Mathews from Port Townsend, Washington, and won the Sutter Home Winery's Build a Better Burger 2005 award for Best Alternative Burgers. Ellie is the author of *The Ungarnished Truth*, in which she describes her experience before and after winning the $1,000,000 Grand Prize in the venerable Pillsbury Bake-Off.

Ground chicken thigh meat or dark meat turkey can be substituted for the pork in these flavorful yet easy burgers. **Serves 6**

Mayonnaise

3/4 cup mayonnaise
1/4 cup finely chopped fresh Thai basil
1/4 cup finely chopped fresh cilantro leaves
1/4 cup finely chopped green onions, including green tops
2 tablespoons freshly squeezed lime juice

Patties

1/4 cup Vietnamese fish sauce (nuoc nam)
4 teaspoons palm sugar or light brown sugar
1 teaspoon Sriracha or other Asian chile sauce
2 pounds ground pork
1/4 cup chunky peanut butter
2 teaspoons grated fresh ginger
2 teaspoons minced garlic
1/2 teaspoon ground star anise

6 rectangular French sandwich rolls, split
6 interior butter lettuce leaves

Prepare a medium-hot fire in a charcoal grill with a cover, or preheat a gas grill to medium high.

To make the mayonnaise, combine all the ingredients in a bowl and mix well. Cover and refrigerate until assembling the burgers.

To make the patties, place the fish sauce, sugar, and chile sauce in a large bowl and mix well. Add the pork, peanut butter, ginger, garlic, and star anise. Handling the meat as little as possible to avoid compacting it, mix well. Form the mixture into 6 equal oblong patties to fit the rolls.

Brush the grill rack with vegetable oil. Place the patties on the rack, cover, and cook, turning once, until done to preference, about 4 minutes on each side for medium. During the last few minutes of cooking, place the rolls, cut side down, on the outer edges of the rack to toast lightly.

To assemble the burgers, spread the roll bottoms with a thin layer of the mayonnaise. On each roll bottom, place a lettuce leaf, a patty, and a generous dollop of the mayonnaise. Add the roll tops and serve.

Red Curry Rice Noodles

Bottled or canned Thai curry paste and fish sauce can be found in the Asian sections of many supermarkets or in Asian markets. **Serves 6**

Sauce

1 (13.5-ounce) can coconut milk
1 roasted red bell pepper, peeled, seeded, and coarsely chopped
1/2 fresh red bell pepper, coarsely chopped
1/2 stalk lemongrass, cut into 2-inch pieces
2 sprigs fresh mint
1 tablespoon minced fresh ginger
1 1/2 teaspoons fish sauce (nuoc nam)
1 tablespoon Thai red curry paste
Kosher or coarse sea salt

Dressing

1/4 cup freshly squeezed lime juice
2 tablespoons slivered fresh ginger
2 teaspoons minced garlic
1 tablespoon sugar
3 tablespoons fish sauce (nuoc nam)
1 teaspoon soy sauce
2 tablespoons peanut oil
1 tablespoon Asian sesame oil

1 pound rock shrimp
1 pound fresh thin rice noodles, or 8 ounces dried very thin rice noodles
1/2 cup whole fresh cilantro leaves
1/2 cup chopped green onions, including green tops
1/2 cup chopped roasted peanuts

To make the sauce, combine the coconut milk, bell peppers, lemongrass, mint, ginger, fish sauce, and curry paste in a saucepan and bring to a boil over medium-high heat. Decrease the heat to maintain a simmer and cook, stirring occasionally, for 1 hour. Remove from the heat, let cool, then transfer to a blender and blend until the mixture is fairly smooth. Pour through a fine-mesh strainer into a bowl; extract all the liquid by pressing the mixture with the back of a spoon. Discard the solids. Season to taste with salt. Cover and refrigerate until chilled.

To make the dressing, combine all the ingredients in a small bowl and whisk to blend well. Cover and refrigerate until chilled.

Bring a pot of salted water to a boil, and then decrease the heat to maintain a simmer. Add the shrimp and cook just until the shrimp turn opaque, about 30 seconds; be careful not to overcook. Drain, rinse with cold water to halt the cooking, and drain again. Transfer to a bowl and toss with a little of the dressing to coat. Cover and refrigerate until chilled.

Place the noodles in a bowl, cover with hot water, and let stand, stirring occasionally, until fresh noodle strands can be separated, about 5 minutes, or until dried noodles are softened, about 15 minutes. Drain well.

Meanwhile, bring a pot of water to boil. Add the noodles and cook, stirring frequently, until tender yet firm to the bite, 1 to 2 minutes. Drain, rinse with cold water, and drain again well.

To serve, combine the noodles and shrimp in a bowl and toss with the remaining dressing. Mound the noodles on a serving platter and ladle the sauce around them. Scatter the cilantro, green onions, and peanuts over the noodles.

Cucumber–Mushroom Salad *with Tangerine Vinaigrette*

The dark Chinese mushrooms commonly known by their Japanese name, *shiitake*, are not grown in Southeast Asia, but dried ones are very popular in the region. Fresh mushrooms provide a wonderful texture and flavor in this refreshing salad. **Serves 6**

8 large shiitake mushrooms
2 tablespoons unseasoned rice vinegar
1 tablespoon soy sauce
1 tablespoon sugar
2 tablespoons peeled and thinly sliced fresh ginger
$^1/_2$ cup water

Vinaigrette
$^1/_4$ cup freshly squeezed tangerine juice
2 tablespoons freshly squeezed lime juice
1 tablespoon unseasoned rice vinegar
1 tablespoon palm sugar or light brown sugar
2 teaspoons fish sauce (nuoc nam)
$^1/_2$ teaspoon Asian chile sauce
2 tablespoons Asian sesame oil
2 tablespoons vegetable oil

1 carrot, peeled and julienned
2 English cucumbers, cut in half lengthwise, seeded, and sliced diagonally $^1/_8$ inch thick
$^1/_4$ cup thinly sliced green onions, including green tops
Kosher or coarse sea salt
1 teaspoon toasted sesame seed

Remove the stems from the mushrooms. Combine the vinegar, soy sauce, sugar, ginger, and water in a pan large enough to hold the mushrooms in a single layer. Bring to a simmer over medium heat and add the mushrooms. Cover, adjust the heat to maintain a simmer, and cook for 5 minutes. Uncover, turn the mushrooms over, cover again, and continue simmering until the mushrooms are tender, about 5 minutes longer. Remove from the heat, uncover, and let the mushrooms cool completely in the braising liquid.

To make the vinaigrette, combine the tangerine juice, lime juice, vinegar, sugar, fish sauce, and chile sauce in a small bowl and whisk to blend well. Add the oils and whisk until emulsified.

Slice the mushrooms into $^1/_8$-inch slices and transfer to a bowl. Add the carrot, cucumbers, and green onions and mix well. Add the vinaigrette and toss to coat. Taste and add more salt, vinegar, fish sauce, and chile sauce, if desired. Cover and refrigerate until chilled.

To serve, transfer the salad to a serving bowl and sprinkle with the sesame seed.

Coconut Tapioca *with Tropical Fruits*

Refreshingly light after a hearty burger meal, this pudding is traditionally served with a mixture of fruit. Consider fresh or canned young coconut, jackfruit, longan, lychee, mango, papaya, pineapple, rambutan, and other tropical fruits. You may find some of the more exotic fruits fresh or canned in Asian markets. Chilling and not shaking the canned coconut milk allows the cream to rise and harden at the top of the can. **Serves 6**

3/4 cup small pearl (not instant or quick-cooking) tapioca

2 1/4 cups water

1/2 cup sugar

Pinch of salt

1 (13.5-ounce) can coconut milk, well chilled and unshaken

1 1/2 cups cut-up assorted tropical fruits (see recipe introduction), chilled

2 teaspoons toasted sesame seed (optional)

Pesticide-free, nontoxic small orchids, for garnish (optional)

Rinse the tapioca well in a mesh strainer under cold running water. Drain and transfer to a saucepan. Add the water, sugar, and salt and stir well. Bring just to a boil over medium-high heat, stirring constantly, then decrease the heat so that the tapioca barely simmers. Cook, stirring occasionally, until the tapioca turns translucent and is tender when tasted, about 15 minutes. Do not overcook or the tapioca will be too thick and sticky. Remove from the heat.

Open the coconut milk without shaking the can. Scoop 3/4 cup of coconut cream from the top of the milk and stir it into the warm pudding. (Cover the remaining coconut milk and refrigerate for another purpose.) Let the pudding cool to room temperature before serving.

To serve, stir the chilled fruits into the pudding and then spoon into 6 individual dishes. Sprinkle each serving with toasted sesame seeds and garnish with orchids.

Southwest Fiesta
Border Food Feast

If you love the *picante* food of the American Southwest and Mexico, along with the bright colors and festive music of the region, this is a party for you.

To create a fun atmosphere, cover the table with a colorful Mexican serape or southwestern Indian blanket, and set it with large terra-cotta pottery dishes, sturdy goblets, and bold flatware. Pick up one or more colors of the serape for the napkins. As a centerpiece, consider filling a big terra-cotta pitcher or pot with an explosion of brightly hued zinnias. *Ristras*, strings of dried red chiles woven together with twine and sisal, are ubiquitous decorations throughout the Southwest and provide a perfect finishing touch to the party setting.

Jeffrey was the opening sous chef at Mark Miller's famed Coyote Café in Santa Fe, so he called on his passion for southwestern foods to create the savory side dishes that complement the winning burger for our fiesta. It may prove a challenge not to overindulge in his fabulous version of *queso fundido* so that you save room for the well-seasoned chicken burgers. James learned the local secret of using canned milks to make rich and smooth flans and was introduced to *cajeta,* caramelized goat's milk, during an extended stay in Santa Fe while writing a book on corn.

Linda Ronstadt's albums *Canciones de mi Padre* and *Mas Canciones* are a perfect accompaniment to the fiesta atmosphere, as are recordings of mariachi bands.

MENU

Sangria

Queso Fundido

Avocado-Tomatillo Salsa

Tortilla Chips

Albuquerque Chicken Burgers
with Jicama Slaw and Chile Cream

Grilled Corn Adobo with
Queso Añejo

Cilantro Slaw *with Creamy Chile-Lime Dressing*

Sutter Home Sauvignon Blanc
Sutter Home White Zinfandel

Cajeta Flans

Sutter Home Moscato

Sangria

Grand Marnier or another premium orange liqueur may be used in place of the Mexican product in this simple yet refreshing blend. **Serves 6**

2 oranges, halved lengthwise, seeded, and cut into $1/4$-inch slices

2 lemons, halved lengthwise, seeded, and cut into $1/4$-inch slices

4 limes, halved lengthwise, seeded, and cut into $1/4$-inch slices

$1/2$ cup sugar

2 (750-ml) bottles Sutter Home Merlot or Zinfandel

$1/2$ cup Mexican orange liqueur, such as Citrónge

Ice cubes, for serving

Fresh orange, lemon, and lime slices, for garnish

Combine the citrus slices and sugar in a pitcher and muddle with the back of a wooden spoon. Add the wine and liqueur and stir until the sugar is dissolved. Taste and add more sugar, if desired. Cover and refrigerate for at least 4 hours.

To serve, pour over ice in wine glasses and garnish with citrus slices.

Queso Fundido

Mexican chorizo and melting cheeses can be found in the refrigerated sections of many major supermarkets or in Latin markets. If you can't locate the Mexican cheeses, substitute Monterey Jack or Cheddar or both. **Serves 6**

4 ounces Mexican chorizo, casing discarded

$3/4$ cup finely chopped white onion

1 cup seeded and finely chopped ripe tomato

2 poblano chiles, roasted, peeled, seeded, and finely chopped

1 teaspoon dried Mexican oregano

$1/2$ cup Sutter Home Sauvignon Blanc

3 cups (about 9 ounces) grated Mexican melting cheese, such as asadero, Chihuahua, or Manchego (not the hard Spanish version)

2 tablespoons coarsely chopped fresh cilantro

Tortilla chips, for serving

Preheat the oven to 300°F.

Combine the chorizo and onion in a nonstick sauté pan or skillet and cook over medium heat, stirring and breaking up the chorizo into small pieces, until nicely browned, about 7 minutes. Stir in the tomato, chiles, and oregano and cook for 2 minutes. Add the wine and cook for 2 minutes longer.

Transfer the mixture to an 8-inch shallow casserole or baking dish and stir in the grated cheese. Bake in the oven until the cheese just melts, about 3 minutes.

Sprinkle with the cilantro and serve immediately with tortilla chips.

Avocado–Tomatillo Salsa

Creamy avocado mellows the tartness of the tomatillos and balances the heat of the chiles in this eye-catching bright green salsa. Bring on the chips! **Serves 6**

1 pound tomatillos, husked, rinsed, and quartered
2/3 cup water
2/3 cup fresh cilantro leaves
1/2 cup coarsely chopped white onion
1 tablespoon coarsely chopped serrano chiles
1 small ripe avocado
1 tablespoon freshly squeezed lime juice
1 teaspoon kosher or coarse sea salt
Tortilla chips, for serving

Combine the tomatillos and water in a saucepan. Bring to a simmer over medium heat, then adjust the heat to maintain a simmer and cook, stirring occasionally, until the tomatillos are very tender when pierced with a knife or skewer, about 10 minutes. Remove from the heat and let cool. Transfer the tomatillos and liquid to a food processor or blender, add the cilantro, onion, and chiles, and blend until smooth. Refrigerate until chilled.

Just before serving, scoop the avocado flesh into the tomatillo mixture and blend until smooth. Add the lime juice and salt and mix well. Taste and add more lime juice and salt, if desired. Transfer to a serving bowl and serve with the tortilla chips.

Albuquerque Chicken Burgers *with Jicama Slaw and Chile Cream*

Harold Cohen, a retired surgeon from Hollywood, Florida, was awarded the First Runner-Up Award for Alternative Burgers at the 2007 Sutter Home Winery's Build a Better Burger Cook-Off for these chicken burgers bursting with southwestern flavor. Harold prefers ancho, a dried poblano, chile for the burgers. It is the sweetest of all dried chiles and the variety most commonly used in Mexico. If you can't locate ground ancho, look for whole ancho chiles in Mexican markets and grind them in a spice grinder, or substitute another ground dried chile. **Serves 6**

Cream
1 cup sour cream
1 1/2 teaspoons ground dried chile, preferably ancho

Slaw
3/4 cup thinly shredded green cabbage
3/4 cup julienned jicama
1/2 cup julienned red peppers
2 tablespoons chopped fresh cilantro leaves
2 tablespoons freshly squeezed lime juice

Patties
2 pounds ground chicken thigh meat
2 teaspoons minced garlic
2 teaspoons dried Mexican oregano
1 teaspoon ground cumin
1/2 teaspoon ground cloves
1 1/2 teaspoons kosher or coarse sea salt
1/2 teaspoon freshly ground black pepper

6 onion rolls, split
1 1/2 cups (about 6 ounces) crumbled Cotija cheese (aged Mexican cheese, sometimes labeled queso añejado)

Prepare a medium-hot fire in a charcoal grill with a cover, or preheat a gas grill to medium high.

To make the cream, combine the ingredients in a small bowl and mix well. Cover and refrigerate until assembling the burgers.

To make the slaw, combine all the ingredients in a bowl and mix well.

To make the patties, combine all the ingredients in a large bowl. Handling the meat as little as possible to avoid compacting it, mix well. Form the mixture into 6 equal patties to fit the rolls.

Brush the grill rack with vegetable oil. Place the patties on the rack, cover, and cook, turning once, just until the juices run clear when the patties are pierced in the center, about 4 minutes per side. During the last few minutes of cooking, place the rolls, cut side down, on the outer edges of the rack to toast lightly.

To assemble the burgers, spread a generous amount of the cream on the cut sides of the rolls. On each roll bottom, place a patty, some crumbled cheese, and some slaw. Add the roll tops and serve.

Grilled Corn Adobo *with Queso Añejo*

A bit of fiery smoked chipotle chile, zesty lime, and pungent toasted cumin mixed with garlicky butter add lots of flavor to ordinary corn on the cob, and a final coating of aged cheese turns the treat into a fiesta! Freely substitute for the *queso añejo* another hard Mexican cheese that can be grated, such as *cotija* or *enchilado*. If none is available, use an Italian Romano. **Serves 6**

6 ears sweet summer corn in husks

1 teaspoon cumin seed

1/2 cup (1 stick) unsalted butter, at room temperature

1 teaspoon finely grated fresh lime zest

2 tablespoons freshly squeezed lime juice

1 canned chipotle chile in adobo, finely chopped

2 tablespoons adobo sauce from canned chipotle chiles

2 teaspoons minced garlic

1/2 teaspoon kosher or coarse sea salt

1 1/2 cups (about 6 ounces) grated queso añejo

2 limes, cut into wedges, for serving

Prepare a medium fire in a charcoal grill with a cover, or preheat a gas grill to medium.

Carefully pull back the husks from the corn and remove the silk. Tie the pulled-back husks into a knot.

Put the cumin seed in a small skillet and toast over medium heat, shaking the pan frequently, just until fragrant, 1 to 2 minutes. Pour onto a plate to cool, then transfer to a spice grinder and grind until fine. Combine the cumin, butter, lime zest, lime juice, chile, adobo sauce, garlic, and salt in a small bowl and mix well. Taste and add more salt, if desired.

Put the cheese in a wide shallow bowl or on a rimmed plate.

Place the corn on the grill rack, cover, and cook, turning occasionally, until tender and browned in spots all over, about 10 minutes.

To serve, rub each grilled corn all over with the chile butter and roll in the cheese to coat. Arrange the corn on a serving platter with the lime wedges.

Cilantro Slaw *with Creamy Chile-Lime Dressing*

Slaw is a perfect addition, on a burger or along-side or both, and here's a southwestern version to add to your cook-out menus. **Serves 6**

Dressing
1/2 cup mayonnaise

1/4 cup sour cream

1 teaspoon finely grated fresh lime zest

2 tablespoons freshly squeezed lime juice

1 tablespoon minced canned or pickled jalapeño chiles

1 tablespoon Dijon mustard

1 teaspoon sugar

1/2 teaspoon kosher or coarse sea salt

1/4 teaspoon freshly ground black pepper

3 cups thinly shredded green cabbage

3 cups thinly shredded red cabbage

1 cup fresh cilantro leaves

1/2 cup chopped red bell pepper (medium-size pieces)

2 tablespoons thinly sliced green onion, including green tops

1/2 cup coarsely chopped dried cherries

1/2 cup roasted shelled pumpkin seed (pepitas)

To make the dressing, combine all the ingredients in a bowl and whisk to blend well. Taste and add more chile, salt, and pepper, if desired. Cover and refrigerate until well chilled.

Combine the cabbages, cilantro, bell pepper, and green onion in a large bowl. Cover and refrigerate until serving.

To serve, toss the slaw with the dressing to coat. Add the cherries and half of the pumpkin seed and toss again. Transfer to a serving bowl and top with the remaining pumpkin seed.

Cajeta Flans

Instead of using the traditional but sometimes tricky process of caramelizing sugar to line the mold, these rich and satiny custards are baked in individual molds containing a spoonful of *cajeta*, a thick caramel sauce made from goat's milk that is popular in the Southwest and Mexico. If you can't locate *cajeta* in a supermarket or Latin market, look for *dulce de leche*, a similar product made from cow's milk, or use any thick caramel sauce.

Serves 6

6 tablespoons prepared cajeta
3 whole eggs
4 egg yolks
1 (14-ounce) can sweetened condensed milk
1 (12-ounce) can evaporated milk, preferably goat's milk
2 teaspoons pure vanilla extract
1/8 teaspoon salt

Preheat the oven to 325°F.

Spoon 1 tablespoon of *cajeta* into each of 6 (6-ounce) ovenproof custard cups or ramekins and swirl to coat the bottom of each cup.

Combine the eggs and egg yolks in a large bowl and whisk until smooth. Add the condensed and evaporated milks, vanilla, and salt and whisk until well blended. Pour through a fine-mesh strainer into a pitcher or large liquid measuring cup and discard the solids. Then pour the mixture into the custard cups, dividing evenly.

Place the custard cups in a large roasting pan, transfer the pan to the oven, and pour hot (not boiling) water into the pan to reach halfway up the sides of the cups. Bake until the custards are barely set in the center, about 50 minutes. Remove the cups from the water bath to a countertop and let cool completely. Then cover and refrigerate until chilled, about 2 hours.

To serve, run a small, sharp knife around the inside edge of a custard cup. Place a serving plate upside down over the cup and invert the cup onto it. Shake the plate a few times to loosen the custard from the cup and then lift off the cup. Repeat with the remaining custards and serve.

Summer and Smoke
Southern Garden Party Barbecue

Lazy summer afternoons and smoke rising from the grill are a natural combination, and the South has a long tradition of summer barbecues. Remember Scarlett O'Hara at the barbecue at Twelve Oaks?

To evoke a bit of southern charm, position a table on the lawn or in a cool, shady spot and set it with white or pastel linens, floral china, crystal goblets, and silver flatware. Finish with a bouquet of pastel garden blossoms or a shallow bowl of floating gardenias.

Southerners enjoy a range of music styles, especially homegrown country, blues, and gospel performed by southern musicians. Consider artists and groups like Alabama, Johnny Cash, Ray Charles, Gladys Knight, Jerry Lee Lewis, Loretta Lynn, Tim McGraw, Dolly Parton, and the Squirrel Nut Zippers.

Our decadent southern menu is built around burgers that are topped with tangy green tomatoes, bacon-laced slaw, and pimento cheese, one of the South's greatest contributions to the culinary world. No cookout from Texas to the Carolinas would be complete without some version of baked beans and pickles, so Jeffrey has put his own spin on those classics here. Southern sweets are legendary, and James reached back to his Louisiana hometown for his mother's old-fashioned cobbler recipe to end this spread, but he couldn't resist adding a touch of his adopted California home to the dish.

MENU

Crab and Cucumber Canapés

Sweet Tea

Sutter Home Sauvignon Blanc

Palmetto Pride Pimento-Cheese Burgers *with Tangy Bacon Slaw and Spicy Grilled Green Tomatoes*

Southern Baked Beans

Honey-Mustard Pickled Beets

Sutter Home Chardonnay
Sutter Home White Merlot
Sutter Home Merlot

Ginger Peachy Cobbler

Sutter Home Moscato

Crab and Cucumber Canapés

Crisp cucumber takes the place of bread slices in these bite-size appetizers with a bit of nostalgia for old-time garden parties. Use the best and freshest crabmeat possible. **Serves 6**

6 ounces fresh lump crabmeat, picked free of shells and cartilage

2 tablespoons mayonnaise

1 tablespoon freshly squeezed lemon juice

1 tablespoon freshly squeezed lime juice

1 tablespoon minced fresh chives

1 teaspoon minced fresh chervil, summer savory, or tarragon

1/4 teaspoon kosher or coarse sea salt

1/4 teaspoon freshly ground black pepper

18 (1/4-inch-thick) slices peeled English cucumber, chilled

Finely grated fresh lemon zest, for garnish

Chop or shred any large pieces of crabmeat. Combine the crabmeat, mayonnaise, lemon juice, lime juice, chives, chervil, salt, and pepper in a bowl and mix to blend. Taste and add more salt and pepper, if desired. Cover and refrigerate until serving (no longer than a few hours).

To serve, drain off any excess juice from the crab mixture. Place a heaping teaspoonful onto each cucumber slice, sprinkle with lemon zest, and arrange on a serving plate.

Sweet Tea

No southern gathering would be complete without plenty of the favorite beverage of the region, preferably made with orange pekoe teabags. It's been said that southerners like a little tea with their sugar. Our version is not supersweet, but feel free to adjust it to your taste; just be sure to add the sugar to the hot brew so that it dissolves quickly. **Serves 6**

2 quarts cold water

3 "family-size" black tea bags, or 12 regular-size tea bags

1/2 cup sugar

2 quarts ice cubes

Additional ice cubes, for serving

Lemon wedges or fresh mint sprigs or both, for serving

Put the water in a large stainless-steel or other nonreactive saucepan. Add the teabags, cover, place over medium heat, and bring just to a bare simmer, about 12 minutes; do not allow to boil. Remove from the heat and let steep, covered, for 2 to 3 minutes.

Put the ice cubes in a heatproof 3-quart pitcher.

Stir the sugar into the tea and pour through a fine-mesh strainer (to remove the bags and any loose leaves from bags that may have split during heating) into the pitcher of ice cubes; to prevent bitterness, do not squeeze or press the tea bags. Stir until the ice melts. Cover and refrigerate.

To serve, place ice cubes in the glasses and add tea. Offer lemon wedges or mint.

Palmetto Pride Pimento-Cheese Burgers
with Tangy Bacon Slaw and Spicy Grilled Green Tomatoes

You don't get more southern than slaw, pimento cheese, and green tomatoes, all of which are included in this homage to the American South from Mary Thompson, of Lexington, South Carolina, who was a finalist in Sutter Home Winery's 2008 Build a Better Burger Cook-Off.

Look for zesty Creole seasoning blends in the spice sections of most major supermarkets; Tony Chachere's and Zatarain's are two popular and widely distributed versions. Cajun seasoning blends made by McCormick and others are very similar and may be substituted. **Serves 6**

Grilled Green Tomatoes
6 (1/2-inch-thick) slices large green tomatoes
Light olive oil, for brushing
Creole seasoning blend, for sprinkling

Slaw
6 slices applewood-smoked bacon
3/4 cup apple cider vinegar
1/4 cup water
1/3 cup firmly packed light brown sugar
1 teaspoon cornstarch
2 cups thinly shredded green cabbage
2 cups finely sliced Vidalia or other sweet onions

Patties
2 pounds ground chuck
2 teaspoons minced garlic
2 teaspoons finely chopped shallots
2 tablespoons Sutter Home Merlot
2 teaspoons kosher or coarse sea salt
1/2 teaspoon dry mustard
1/2 teaspoon freshly ground white pepper

Pimento Cheese
1 1/2 cups (about 4 1/2 ounces) coarsely grated sharp Cheddar cheese
1 1/2 cups (about 4 1/2 ounces) coarsely grated Vermont white Cheddar cheese
3 ounces jarred pimentos, drained and diced
3 ounces cream cheese, softened
3 tablespoons mayonnaise

6 soft Kaiser rolls, split

Prepare a medium-hot fire in a charcoal grill with a cover, or preheat a gas grill to medium high.

To prepare the tomatoes, brush both sides of the tomato slices with oil and sprinkle both sides liberally with Creole seasoning. Set aside.

To make the slaw, cook the bacon on the grill in a heavy fireproof skillet until crisp. Transfer to paper towels to drain. Discard the bacon grease from the skillet and return it to the heat. Pour the vinegar and water into the skillet and whisk until the liquid begins to simmer. Add the brown sugar and cornstarch and continue to whisk while simmering until the mixture begins to thicken slightly and reduce, 4 to 5 minutes. Add the cabbage and onions and sauté for 2 to 3 minutes. Using a large slotted spoon, transfer the hot slaw mixture to a bowl. Crumble the bacon and place in small bowl. Set aside until assembling the burgers.

To make the patties, combine all the ingredients in a large bowl. Handling the meat as little as possible to avoid compacting it, mix well. Form the mixture into 6 equal patties to fit the rolls.

continued

Palmetto Pride Pimento-Cheese Burgers, *continued*

To make the cheese, combine all the ingredients in a bowl and mix until well combined. Divide into 6 equal portions and shape into disks to fit the patties.

Brush the grill rack with vegetable oil. Place the patties on the rack, cover, and cook, turning once, until done to preference, about 5 minutes on each side for medium. While the patties are grilling, place the tomato slices on the grill and cook just until tender, 2 to 3 minutes on each side. During the last few minutes of cooking, place a cheese disk on each patty and cook until soft but not completely melted; also place the buns, cut side down, on the outer edges of the rack to toast lightly.

To assemble the burgers, add the crumbled bacon to the slaw and toss. On each roll bottom, place a slice of grilled tomato, a patty, and some slaw. Add the roll tops and serve.

Let's set the record straight. We know that grilling burgers isn't truly barbecuing, which implies very slow cooking with the indirect heat from a wood fire that produces lots of smoke. Nowadays, however, lots of folks commonly dub anything cooked over charcoal or on a gas grill "barbecue" and call any cookout the same, so enjoy our southern barbecue party in your own backyard.

Southern Baked Beans

While some southern cooks may start with canned pork and beans and "fix 'em up," we've chosen to cook the beans "from scratch" for our version of an American classic. Navy beans are traditional, but you may use other beans; Jeffrey recommends heirloom varieties from Rancho Gordo. **Serves 6**

1 pound dried beans
1 pound sliced bacon, slices cut crosswise into 1/2-inch strips
2 cups finely chopped yellow onions
4 teaspoons coarsely chopped garlic
1 (15-ounce) can tomato sauce
1/2 cup firmly packed dark brown sugar
1/4 cup yellow mustard
1 tablespoon yellow mustard seed
1 teaspoon hot sauce

Spread the beans out on a flat surface and carefully pick them over by hand to remove any foreign bits or imperfect beans. Place the beans in a colander and rinse well with cold water to remove the dust accumulated during drying and storing.

For overnight soaking, put the beans in a bowl and cover with cold water by about 3 inches. Cover the bowl and refrigerate overnight.

For quick soaking, put the beans in a large pot and cover with cold water by about 2 inches. Bring to a boil over medium-high heat and boil for 2 minutes. Remove from the heat and let stand, covered, for 1 hour.

Drain the soaked beans in a colander and rinse with cold water. Rinse out the pot (if used for soaking) and return the beans to it. Add water to cover the beans by 2 inches. Place over medium-high heat and bring just to a boil, using a wire skimmer or slotted spoon to remove any foam from the surface. Decrease the heat to maintain a simmer, cover partially, and simmer until the beans are tender but not mushy; start checking after about 20 minutes, because the timing depends on the variety and freshness of the beans. Drain the beans, reserving 2 cups of the cooking liquid.

Preheat the oven to 325°F.

Cook the bacon in a large Dutch oven or other ovenproof pot over medium heat, stirring occasionally, until most of the fat is rendered, 10 to 15 minutes. With a slotted spoon, remove the bacon to paper towels to drain. Discard all but 2 tablespoons of the bacon fat and return the pot to medium heat. Add the onions and garlic and cook, stirring frequently, until soft, about 5 minutes. Stir in the cooked beans, drained bacon, tomato sauce, sugar, mustard, mustard seeds, hot sauce, and 1 cup of the reserved bean-cooking liquid. Cover the pot with its lid or aluminum foil and bake for 1 hour. Remove the lid and continue baking until thick and lightly browned, about 15 minutes longer; if the beans get dry before they are ready, stir in a little more of the reserved cooking liquid.

> If your time is really limited, substitute 4 (15-ounce) cans of navy beans for the dried ones; drain the canned beans, reserving the liquid, and skip the first 4 paragraphs of the directions.

Honey-Mustard Pickled Beets

A dish of pickles is a must for any southern party, and beets are a favorite. To add color to the menu, use a combination of beet varieties for this "quick pickle" recipe. **Serves 6**

8 fresh beets, 2 to 2$^{1}/_{2}$ inches in diameter
3 tablespoons whole-grain Dijon mustard
3 tablespoons honey
2 tablespoons apple cider vinegar
1 tablespoon finely grated fresh orange zest
2 tablespoons freshly squeezed orange juice
1 tablespoon finely chopped fresh tarragon
$^{1}/_{2}$ teaspoon kosher or coarse sea salt
$^{1}/_{4}$ teaspoon freshly ground black pepper
$^{1}/_{4}$ cup grapeseed or mild olive oil
$^{1}/_{4}$ cup chopped red onion
$^{1}/_{4}$ pound sliced bacon, slices cut crosswise
    into $^{1}/_{8}$-inch strips
$^{1}/_{4}$ cup pecan halves, lightly toasted
$^{1}/_{4}$ cup (about 1 ounce) crumbled mild blue
    cheese

Remove the greens from the beets and reserve for another use. Bring a large pot of water to a boil over high heat and add the beets. Decrease the heat to maintain a simmer, cover partially, and simmer until the beets are tender when pierced with a skewer, 30 minutes to 1 hour, depending on the size and variety of beet. Drain and let cool slightly.

Combine the mustard, honey, vinegar, orange zest, orange juice, tarragon, salt, and pepper in a stainless-steel, glass, or ceramic bowl (the beets may stain a plastic bowl) and whisk to blend well. Add the oil and whisk until emulsified. Taste and add more salt and pepper, if desired.

When the beets are cool enough to handle, peel with a paring knife and cut each into 6 to 8 wedges. Add the beets and onion to the mustard mixture and gently toss to coat. Cover and refrigerate, gently tossing occasionally, for at least 2 hours, to pickle.

Cook the bacon in a skillet over medium heat until browned and crisp. With a slotted spoon remove it to paper towels to drain.

To serve, transfer the pickled beets to a serving bowl and sprinkle with the bacon, pecans, and cheese.

Ginger Peachy Cobbler

The traditional dollops of biscuit dough that look like cobblestones inspired the name of this dessert, but several variations of cobbler are popular with southerners. Here's James's gingery adaptation of the version that his mother often made while he was growing up in Louisiana, in which peaches atop a simple batter migrate to the bottom during the baking. **Serves 6**

1/2 cup (1 stick) butter
1 cup all-purpose flour
1/2 cup granulated sugar
1/4 cup firmly packed light brown sugar
1 1/2 teaspoons baking powder
1/2 teaspoon salt
1 cup milk (not nonfat)
1 teaspoon pure vanilla extract
3 cups peeled and sliced fresh peaches
1/4 cup finely chopped crystallized ginger
Vanilla ice cream or whipped cream,
  for serving
6 fresh mint sprigs, for garnish

Preheat the oven to 350°F. Place the butter in an 8-inch square baking dish and transfer to the oven just until the butter is melted, 2 to 3 minutes.

Meanwhile, combine the flour, granulated sugar, brown sugar, baking powder, and salt in a large bowl and whisk to blend. Stir in the milk and vanilla and whisk until smooth. Slowly pour the batter over the melted butter; do not stir. Scatter the peaches and ginger evenly over the batter.

Bake until batter rises to the top and turns golden brown, 45 to 55 minutes, depending on the juiciness of the peaches. Transfer to a work surface to cool slightly before serving warm.

To serve, scoop the warm cobbler equally into 6 individual bowls and add a small scoop of ice cream or whipped cream to each serving. Garnish with the mint.

ACKNOWLEDGMENTS

To the Trinchero and Torres families, owners of Sutter Home Winery, for the creation and continued support of Build a Better Burger.

To Jeffrey Starr's Trinchero Culinary Center chefs James Houghton and Matthew Bennett for developing and testing many of the side dish recipes.

To Andrew Moore for his invaluable assistance in writing, dessert recipe development, and long hours of testing every recipe.

To the management at Sutter Home Winery for making this book possible, and BBBig thanks to the book team—Michele Ashby, Juliana French-Arnold, Wendy Nyberg, and Andrea Staby—for their numerous contributions to the project.

To Aaron Wehner at Ten Speed Press for seeing value in our book idea, to our editor Melissa Moore and book designer Betsy Stromberg for turning our words and photos into a stylish volume, and to copyeditor Zipporah Collins and proofreader Sharron Wood for polishing our prose.

To photographer Dan Mills for creatively capturing each party, and for making the photography environment so pleasant for everyone involved.

To food stylist Kim Kissling and her assistants Sarah Fairhurst and Tina Stamos and intern Dana Bonagura for making every dish look great.

To prop stylist Joanna Badano for assembling perfect table settings for the parties shot on location.

To Paul Stokey and his staff at Tesoro in St. Helena, California for the fabulous flowers throughout the book.

To Steve and Betsy Moulds for allowing us to Flip 'n' Splash in their fabulous pool.

To Dave and Nancy Yewell for the use of their beautiful vineyard for A Place in the Sun.

To Sam Gittings for sharing his picturesque Blue Tooth barn for our Fall Frolic.

To Judd and Holly Finkelstein for the fun collection of tiki bar items for Burgers in Paradise.

To Negin Kamangar for loaning the silk tenting, props, and costumes for Moroccan Mystique.

To Eric and Leslee Iskin of Olde Towne Jewelers in Santa Rosa, CA for the Burgers and Blues dishes.

To Ada Nourse for the lovely dishes used for A Place in the Sun and Summer and Smoke.

To the partygoers who posed—along with our editorial and photography team—for the photos: Sandi Akers, Paul Carnazola, Lindsay Engel, Judd Finkelstein, Marc Gallo, Tom Gorton, Morgan Gross, Jason Hart, Tara Hensley, Jill Hunting, Josh La Cuzla, Jose Lava, Melissa Lugo, Nora McAuley, Lynda Mulczynski, Laisa Munoz, Omar Navarro, Ricky Reid, David Smith, Megan Steffen, Kyle Stroud, Brad and Julie Swim, Tony Torres, and Sharon Werner.

To the great burger cooks whose winning recipes are featured in this book, and to the many thousands of creative burger enthusiasts for competing in the first 20 years of Build a Better Burger.

INDEX

Library of Congress Cataloging-in-Publication Data is on file with the publisher
ISBN 978-1-58008-110-8

Printed in China

Book design by Betsy Stromberg
Editorial assistance by Andrew Moore
Recipe development and testing assistance by James Houghton, Matthew Bennett, and Andrew Moore
Photography by Dan Mills
Food styling by Kimberly Kissling
Food styling assistance by Sarah Fairhurst and Tina Stamos and intern Dana Bonagura
Prop styling by Joanna Badano (location) and Kimberly Kissling (studio)
Flowers by Tesoro, St. Helena, California

10 9 8 7 6 5 4 3 2 1

First Edition